# Branding and Marketing:

*Practical Step-by-Step Strategies on How to Build your Brand and Establish Brand Loyalty using Social Media Marketing to Gain More Customers and Boost your Business*

Gavin Turner

© **Copyright 2019 by Gavin Turner - All rights reserved.**

The contents of this book may not be reproduced, duplicated, or transmitted without direct written permission from the author.

Under no circumstances will any legal responsibility or blame be held against the publisher for any reparation, damages, or monetary loss due to the information herein, either directly or indirectly.

Legal Notice:

This book is copyright protected; it is only for personal use. You cannot amend, distribute, sell, use, quote, or paraphrase any part of the content within this book without the consent of the author.

Disclaimer Notice:

Please note the information contained within this document is for educational and entertainment purposes only. Every attempt has been made to provide accurate, up to date, and completely reliable information. No warranties of any kind are expressed or implied. Readers acknowledge that the author is not engaging in the rendering of legal, financial, medical, or professional advice. The content of this book has been derived from various sources. Please consult a licensed professional before attempting any techniques outlined in this book.

By reading this document, the reader agrees that under no circumstances is the author responsible for any losses, direct or indirect, which are incurred as a result of the use of the information contained within this document, including, but not limited to, —errors, omissions, or inaccuracies.

# Table of Contents

Introduction

Chapter 1: Getting Started with Branding

Chapter 2: Aligning Branding With Your Business Goals

Chapter 3: Finding and Serving Your Target Customers

Chapter 4: The One Critical Element in your Branding

Chapter 5: Integrating Branding into Content

Chapter 6: Leveraging Social Media Marketing to Help Build your Brand

Chapter 7: Promoting Your Brand with Facebook

Chapter 8: Promoting Your Brand with Instagram

Chapter 9: Promoting Your Brand with YouTube

Chapter 10: Promoting Your Brand with Twitter

Chapter 11: Guide to Creating a Brand Logo

Chapter 12: Building Brand Loyalty

Chapter 13: Putting It All Together - How to Launch A Branding Campaign

Bonus Chapter: When is it Time to Rebrand

Conclusion
References

# Introduction

Picture this: If you are craving for coffee and find yourself walking between a Starbucks on your right and a newly-opened coffee shop on your left, and with all things being equal in terms of quality and price, which shop would you go to for coffee?

Chances are, you'll be walking to your right.

That's how critical a brand is to a business. A brand gives customers that mental shortcut to associations that people are familiar with, usually with positive emotions. Since we tend to buy based on our feelings, those products or services with an established brand have the best likelihood of getting sales.

Brand building is just the beginning of the brand awareness journey; the next phase is to gain brand loyalty among your target audience. The problem is some companies spend less time and effort on the branding aspect. Meanwhile, the companies that recognize the importance of branding and have learned how to best approach their brand building stand out in the marketplace and grow their sales. Some have even flourished spreading their brand awareness across the internet and social media.

If you are thinking about starting your brand or if you have already established one, this book will help you take things to the next level. You might even be someone without a brand or someone who wants to improve, repair, or grow a brand. If you want more customers for your brand, this book will be the perfect how-to guide as well. It will help you to start from scratch and go all the way to develop a valuable brand. This book will provide you with strategies and tactics for brand building and marketing your brand. All the important topics crucial to marketing and branding have been discussed here. You will soon see why new businesses are growing and flourishing much faster than ever before. Such is the power of good branding and effective social media marketing.

You have to understand that branding and

marketing are crucial for a successful business.

- It is essential in paving the way for marketing success. When you hear the name of specific brands, you will automatically think of each in a certain way. This is how companies' brand and market their business. Similarly, your brand name should drive people to think in a positive and directed way as will benefit it. A consumer will think of the brand image according to where they first saw it or even heard of it.
- In this book, you will identify how to portray your vision through your brand image in a way that people always view it positively. You have to build a brand that people trust, love, and want to be loyal to. This book will help to guide you to build a strong brand that stands out.
- You will learn how to leverage social media marketing to help you build your brand and create a strong presence online. The book will provide you with information on how you can use various

- popular social media platforms like Facebook, Instagram, YouTube and Twitter to grow your brand and reach out to a larger target audience.
- A comprehensive guide on launching a successful branding campaign is also provided.

Many people use the words "branding" and "marketing" together like they mean the same thing. However, it makes all the difference in the success of your business if you are aware of the difference between both and understands that they are both important. Branding should precede any effort you make to market your business. Branding is about expressing the value of your business to others by clarifying what the brand is all about. Branding will support the marketing efforts you make for your product or service. Marketing is the effort you make to sell your product or your service. It is essential to understand that branding is more significant than all the marketing tactics you apply over time since it will build brand loyalty and establish your brand image forever. Problems arise when the difference between branding and marketing is not recognized. Your business should involve significant effort in building and developing your brand alongside marketing efforts. The competitive landscape in today's world requires a proactive and consistent effort in order for your business to succeed. Using online marketing strategies like social media marketing play a significant role in this.

What makes this book unique and distinct from others is that it will help you build your brand and market it in a much more modern way. The old branding and marketing strategies are not enough in this digital age, where social media is omnipresent. You have to stay current and move with the times. Here, I have put together various ways in which you can build a unique and strong brand that thrives with the help of social media. As you read through the book, you will understand why social media can make or break your business. You also need to remember that not all social media platforms will be suited to your brand. You have to find what works best for you and then take the necessary steps. Investing your time, effort and money in social media marketing will never be a source of regret for you.

In today's marketplace, the competition is high, and there is a constant shift in the various strategies used by businesses to stay on top of the game. It is vital for every business, including yours, to have this kind of proactive approach to ensure the success of their business.

Don't worry about where you or your brand is at right now. Just take time out to read through this book and use it for your benefit. The strategies that you are about to read will help you identify the exact steps you need to take and also understand why it is vital to do so. It's not that other successful businesses have a completely new or better product or service than what you offer. What makes them successful is that they know the tricks of the trade and have used them to succeed despite all the competition. With this book, you will soon be one of them with an improved brand presence by using the latest marketing strategies that not only target customers but also help build a loyal following, which will make your customers come back to you and your services for years to come.

So let us begin by reading everything you need to know about branding and marketing with social media to help grow your business.

# Chapter 1: Getting Started with Branding

# Chapter 1: Getting Started with Branding

## 1.1 Fundamentals of Branding

Let's begin with a better understanding of what branding is. By definition, it is a part of marketing where the company creates its name or symbol. This brand name or logo will be easily identified and associated with the company it belongs to. When consumers choose a product or service, they will be able to distinguish it from others with the help of the branding. Branding creates a memorable impression that makes it easy for clients to identify your products and know what to expect. You can use branding to distinguish your company from any competitors and clarify to clients that your product or service is better compared to others. When you build your brand, you can use it to be a reflective representation of your business and what it stands for. Branding is not just about creating the logo and having a brand name. Various aspects are involved, and you will learn of all this as you read through the book. All of these are contributing elements in creating a unique brand profile that will grab attention from your targeted consumers.

## 1.2 History and Evolution of Branding

The abstract idea of branding started a hundred years ago or much earlier. To understand branding, we must realize that a brand is not a logo, advertisement, corporate identity, or marketing; it is a sense of belonging, action, security and a unique set of values. The word brand is Germanic in its origin[1], which means to burn. It was derived from the word "Brandr," from Ancient Norse, which also meant to burn. Branding originally started in the 1650s when people began branding cattle for ownership. The brand referred to as burning wood. It was used as a verb only in late English, where it came to mean, "to permanently mark with a hot iron." It was used as a stamp of ownership. Individual

---

[1] Holland, T., & Holland, T. (2019). What Is Branding? A Brief History. Retrieved from https://www.skyword.com/contentstandard/creativity/branding-brief-history/

ranches would have their own set of unique marks that were burned into the skin of animals to show that they belonged to the respected owners; this helped them identify their belonging when stolen or mixed with animals from other ranches. Criminals were also branded as punishments. As horrendous as it may sound today, slaves were also branded during this period to indicate ownership.

Later in the 1800s, branding changed from simply showing ownership to showcasing ownership as an advertisement to everyone. This was the time when there was a rise in mass production and shipments to trade goods. Products like ale and wine started to be produced and distributed to large areas during this period. So, the producers began burning their maker's mark on wine caskets, and wooden cases of goods to distinguish their product from the rest. The branding on these cases was regarded as a guaranteed right product, excellent quality, and a good source. People would buy from these brands and show them to other people, which led to branding ultimately taking another shape. It became a symbol of high quality, and likewise, prices of the higher quality good rose in turn. In the 1870s trademark was registered s[2]o that the competitors did not recreate the same products.

To go deeper into the history of branding,[3] we should know that branding goes back to the Egyptian and the Indus Valley civilization. There are images of branding cattle in Egyptian tombs dated 2700 BCE. Many seals were discovered from the sites of the Harappa civilization dating between (3,300- 1,300 BCE) when local people depended mainly on trade. Seals were introduced in Mesopotamia around 3,000 BCE, and these seals represented labels of goods and ownership of properties. The use of labels of the creator on items such as pots and ceramics were standard branding methods in ancient Greece and Rome.

---

[2] Know, T. (2019). Trademarks: Everything You Need to Know. Retrieved from https://www.upcounsel.com/trademarks

[3] Brand - WikiModern. (2019). Retrieved from https://wikimodern.com/en/Brand_name

These ancient societies were strict when it came to the quality of products, so they conveyed the genuineness of a product through branding during that time by attaching stone or clay seals bearing pressed images of the owner's personal identity most times. Most historians suggest that the thumbprints used in potteries that were one of the most popular pictorial brands must be termed "photo-brands." They do not agree that these seals can be comparable with modern branding. Archaeological evidence of stamps and seals, which were used on pottery, bricks, storage containers, and ceramics were discovered across the Roman Empire. These types of markings were common in ancient Greece by the 6th Century BCE.[4]

One of the oldest maker's mark or brand was found in India dating back to the Vedic period (ca. 1,100 to 500 BCE) an herbal paste called Chyawanprash known for its health benefits. Another very early example of a popular product

---

[4] Cartwright, M., & Cartwright, M. (2019). Ancient Greek Pottery. Retrieved from https://www.ancient.eu/Greek_Pottery/

is White Rabbit, which dates back to the Chinese Song Dynasty[5] (960- 1127 CE). The copper plate had a trademark of a white rabbit crushing herbs. A white rabbit also symbolizes good luck. These plates were primarily relevant to women who were the principal purchasers. The use of such marks on various products declined with the Roman Empire. However, by the 13th-century, branding had become a crucial aspect in specific types of goods, and by the 1200s brands on bread became a compulsion in England.

Different types of branding like hallmarks, silver maker's mark, pottery maker's mark, stamps, and watermarks were widely used during this period across Europe. Branding was later all about perception. It was about creating, managing, and building a widespread perception of the market place. The more that people perceive you or your company in a particular way, the more powerful and valuable

---

[5] Eckhardt, G. M., & Bengtsson, A. (2010). A Brief History of Branding in China. *Journal of Macromarketing, 30*(3), 210–221. https://doi.org/10.1177/0276146709352219

your brand. One of the prime examples of a brand is Coca-Cola, which is a big business right now valued at 198.58 billion dollars in 2019, which is more than the total GDP of many small countries combined. In 1886 only nine bottles were sold, and today, more than 1.9 billion servings of Coca-Cola are sold in more than 200 countries each day. The rise in mass media created different ways to create demand for products. Televisions and radios helped manufactures announce their products. Many things can be branded such as products, services, places, religion as well as people.

Brands, however, work differently in this world at the moment because of the rise of the Internet and social media, which are stirring a path for the evolution of branding. Social media brands like Google and Facebook rely solely on their customers/users to help construct their value. Google is the number one search engine, where you will be informed of almost anything in the world, so it is widely popular and is perceived well by the public. YouTube is another brand that connects you with a different environment, knowledge, and films altogether. Brands like eBay or Amazon let you sell items as well as buy items. Facebook is a brand that allows you to connect with old friends as well as make new friends. Skype makes you feel that the world is so small, just a click and you can connect through video calls with people who are miles and miles apart from you. Wikipedia is another powerful brand that is leading on the Internet, which has information and provides knowledge to all. Say the name and virtually everyone in the world will respond with the same adjective or emotions. Individual or people brands are brands like The Beatles who were a musical group. People perceived their music as one of the best in the music industry. Brands like Apple are other prominent examples of individual branding-Steve Jobs being the face of Apple. Eateries like KFC are other big individual brands in today's world.

Branding emerged to ensure honesty, identify ownership, differentiate the quality of the product, and create an emotional bond. Despite how the meaning of branding something has broadened and changed over the years, almost all of the older ways and kinds of branding are still widely used today. But history does provide insight into modern branding.

## 1.3 Understanding Marketing

By definition, marketing involves the actions you take to promote and sell your products or services. It includes market research and different types of advertising. However, there is no exact way to define marketing since it has various facets and can be all-encompassing. Marketing overlaps with advertising and sales quite a bit. Some may wonder why marketing is such a necessary component in product development, sales pitches, or even retail distribution, but you will understand why it is essential. A marketing expert has a firm grasp of consumer personas. They take time to research and analyze consumers using surveys, focus groups, etc. Marketing requires proper knowledge of what the consumers want and to figure out how your business can appeal to them. Marketing is the method by which you can create interest in what your company offers. Marketing is related to every aspect of your business, starting from product development to distribution or sales. This book will help you understand and learn how modern marketing can benefit your brand.

## 1.4 Marketing over the Years

The practice of marketing has been carried out for fifteen thousand years. It all began with humble beginnings of simply trying to sell services and goods. With the beginning of trade, people did not have all the technologies that we have today, but they were still able to market their products. And because of trade, consumerism is what it is today. People traded products such as spices and material through promotions such as word of mouth. Some historians believe that it all started with trying to trade goods in a certain way. Marketing is all about persuasion and using the right message and delivery method at just the right time. Although in ancient times this activity may not have been recognized as marketing, this is where the idea of marketing started developing. Marketing was not an acknowledged study until the 1900s. It played an essential role throughout history.

For a better grasp of how it works, let's look back to the beginning of time. Cave dwellers used charcoal drawings informing others about things like dinosaur, rocks and fire demonstrations and creating the wheel. The con to this, however, was that messages were not portable and you had to be physically present there to understand the storytelling of those cave drawing. Fast forward a few thousand years, in 1450 Johannes Gutenberg invented the printing press. This was marketing's first big break allowing mass production of marketing and advertising materials[6]. It enabled people to spread the news about their business throughout the cities by the masses. This is why Gutenberg is considered by many as the king of

---

[6] History of advertising: No 130: Johann Gutenberg's printing press. (2019). Retrieved from https://www.campaignlive.co.uk/article/history-advertising-no-130-johann-gutenbergs-printing-press/1344881

mass communication. But there was a problem, much of the target market could not read, which significantly limited the market. In 1836 the first paid advertisement was released; this is what started the advertisements in newspapers that we see to this day. In the 1730s magazines came into existence, which was used as an advertisement source. Posters were the next steps in the growth of marketing when people hung posters of products or anything they wanted to sell by the end of the 1830s.

The next invention was the electromagnetic telegraph invented circa 1840. Wang Samuel Morse created his language, Morse Code, words from one transmitter could travel far away; the problem was that only a few people could understand what came out on the other end! Also, it is said that people used telegrams to send spam and the earliest recorded telegraph spam was in 1864. Billboards became famous in 1867 when people started renting billboards for weeks or even months for advertising purposes. Then came the 1900s when CRM (Customer Relationship Management) was developed. This is where customer satisfaction was evaluated through surveys and all the items sold were tracked to determine how well the product was selling, which became essential to marketing and market research. In the 1920s, Radio came into existence and businesses started advertising on radios. At the beginning of 1940, after the invention of television, there was a lot of marketing commercials. During the 1950-1960 the telephone came into existence and mass marketing was finally here. Telemarketing was born. The problem was that everyone got interrupted during dinner because the phone would ring with messages about selling and buying goods.

The golden age of marketing arrived when the internet came into existence. That is when websites, blogging, and article marketing, email, social media, SEO, etc. started to exist. The search market came into existence in 1995, and businesses began promoting themselves by sending traffic to a website from search engines. They also started utilizing SEO to drive traffic to websites by using keywords typed by the consumers in the search engines. Blogging was another form of marketing that began shortly after this in 1998. Businesses, as well as individuals, started creating blogs to share their business information or their brand or interest, and this was a turning point in the history of marketing. In early 2000, Pay-per-click surfaced within the Internet marketing place. This was a technique where the company would pay a small fee for every click on a specific advertisement.

Social Media marketing developed around 2003. Social media became a popular way for people to share ideas with others; therefore, there was a niche for social media marketing. In 2005 Google Analytics came into existence. This gave users of Google websites information on how many audiences they had reached on a specific day.

Finally, cross-media-marketing and data mining arrived. Cross-media marketing involves various media forms to assimilate marketing messages to people's consciousness.

Using a variety of media would mean putting out information to many consumers, cross-marketing utilizing a combination of different search engines, mobile apps, link ads, commercials on YouTube as well as television, YouTube videos, trade show marketing, etc. Many forms of cross-marketing are so subtle that often customers don't realize that they see marketing. Data mining is gathering particular information to unlock the secrets of each individual's likes, dislikes, and preferences. Understanding what the data reveals is a science in itself now. The advantage of using this data property is that it provides a benefit to the marketer when tailoring the message and choosing the marketing vehicle when the prospect is almost ready to purchase. Cross-channel marketing is knowing your audience's preferences so that you can deliver the right message on the right platform at the right time. The advantage of cross-channel marketing is that it streamlines the process; it minimizes cost and improves conversion rates. The foundational principle in cross-media marketing is to spread your brand across as many social media platforms as possible. Nearly every business uses at least two forms of social media to market themselves. Data mining is another potent weapon in terms of marketing as it helps in the process of discovering hidden patterns in a large amount of data. It gathers relevant information useful for the business.

Company data is either non-operational (forecast), transactional (day-to-day sales), inventory and cost, or metadata which is concerned with the logical database. Direct marketing with the use of data mining can help you know who you need to contact. This may be helpful for a person who tweets or a person who uses Linkedin because data enables you to find the person's likes and dislikes, their age, and a boatload of other useful information. This helps to increase organizational revenue with data mining techniques that give a clear picture of strong consumer focus, providing clear information on the product sold, price, customer demographics, and being aware of their competition. It selects a suitable algorithm, which identifies trends in a set of data; the most popular algorithm used is a classification and regression algorithm to determine the relationship between data elements.

Marketing has changed over thousands of years to what we see as marketing today. The overall evolution of marketing has given a rise in the development of business. Marketing has taken different shapes and forms after going through all the changes from the beginning of civilization. The practice of marketing at the start was conservative and lacked information. But after the development of information technology, marketing took a turn to what it is today. The way people do their business and sell or purchase products has changed through the different eras with the evolution of the concept.

The first part of this book covers branding in general, while the second part delves into the marketing aspect. You will learn more about leveraging the power of social media marketing later in the book. It will help you to build your brand and promote it while encouraging brand loyalty among customers.

## 1.5 Why is Branding Essential for Business?

It is crucial that you understand why branding is essential in the first place. In the marketing world, the importance of branding has been a topic of debate in various instances. One reason is that the marketing budget has to be kept in mind. The commitment to branding also requires a commitment to spending more in this department, and some doubt the need for it. However, trust us when we say that branding will be worth every penny you spend on it. That is of course if you do it the right way.

Brand building will have various benefits for your company:

### *Your brand will get recognition*

This is the main reason why branding is essential for your business. Consumers will recognize and get familiar with your business through the brand. The logo plays a crucial role in this because it will act as the face of your company. You need to ensure that it is a powerful and memorable, professional logo.

### *It will increase business value*

If you are thinking in terms of generating future business, branding will help. The branding will give your company more value and leverage. The brand, once firmly established, will be a much more appealing investment opportunity for clients. The power of the brand can be leveraged to enter new segments or different markets, for gaining distribution and also for co-branding.

### *Branding will create customer preference*

A vast variety of products are available across all categories these days. This can create confusion and customers are uncertain about their choices. They deal with this by gravitating towards the brands that they are familiar with and trust. Purchasing from such established brands is what consumers prefer.

### *It will generate new customers consistently*

When you establish a good brand, there will be no issues with generating more customers. The company will already have a good impression on the market, and new consumers will be more likely to buy from a good brand. The brand name will help to create a sense of dependability that appeals to the people. Once you establish the brand properly, the word will spread automatically, and you will see people drifting your way.

### *Branding increases satisfaction and pride among employees*

It is easy to see why employees prefer working for firmly established brands. They are satisfied with their job when they believe in what the brand stands for. It also gives them the pride to work for a company that has a good reputation and is well known. You can increase employee loyalty and productivity in your company when you build up your brand. Giving them merchandise with brand logos also establishes a sense of belonging among them. Your business will flourish when your employees are happy working with you.

## It is easier to overcome minor crises with good branding

Every business is susceptible to highs and lows. But when a well-established brand faces minor problems, it is easier for them to come back and to flourish compared to others and this is due to the confidence and trust that the brand has built among its consumers and clients over the years.

## New competitors are hesitant to enter your market

People are usually reluctant to enter into market segments where some brands dominate. Being among these strong dominant brands will reduce the chances of more competition in the future.

## Profits can increase drastically

One of the attractive benefits of investing in branding is that people will be willing to pay more for your products. If you compare the same product that is being sold without branding, consumers will pay significantly lower prices. So if you want to increase your market price, establish a premium brand.

### *Distributor loyalty increases*

If you think about business for independent distributors, they are only in it for the money. Brand loyalty is not of concern for them individually. However, when their customers are loyal to your brand, they have no choice but to provide according to demand. This reduces the chances of losing distributors for your company.

### *Branding will also aid in attracting new distributors*

You will find it very easy to push your products to new distributors when your brand's consumer loyalty is established. Distributors are always looking for brands that will be popular among customers and will give them a higher turnover.

This summary should help you to realize why

branding is such an essential investment for your business. If you want to advertise, promote, and grow your business, it is crucial to have great branding.

**1.6 How Branding Works**

*Branding works for companies in various ways*

A brand itself is a name, symbol, term, design, or a combination of such elements. This brand helps in the identification of specific goods and services provided by a company and helps to differentiate them from those of competitors. Branding has different components, such as brand logo, symbols, or package designs. The role of a brand can be for consumers, firms, or product roles. Branding allows you to identify where a product comes from, and your brand can take responsibility for any product or service with its name.

Consumers can hold the brand accountable for its products or services. Branding also simplifies the handling of products and makes it easier to organize inventory or accounting records.

Another benefit of branding is that it could offer legal protection for certain unique features of products provided by that brand. Consumers look towards strong brands to provide them with high-quality products that they could repeatedly purchase by trusting in the brand name. It is vital to gain the trust of consumers in order to compete against other brands. Your branding strategy will only be successful if you convince your consumers that there are meaningful differences in the quality of the products you offer compared to your competitors.

To meet the positive impact of branding, you should try to aim for over-delivering while underselling. Also, ensure excellent customer care and regular surveys of feedback from them. Find excuses to interact with potential customers and keep them engaged with your brand. Add personal touches like sending them emails on birthdays and anniversaries. Using the right branding moves will create an organic generation of leads.

Brand awareness will increase with the help of online reviews and any mentions on social media. Branding will help you get maximum customers with little effort, so don't focus solely on numbers or revenue. Invest time in building a strong personality for your brand that the public can identify with.

**Your Quick Start Action Step:**

Step 1: Firstly, we recommend that you visit some websites to learn more about branding. It will help you get a better understanding that you can apply while implementing branding for your business.

Step 2: Determine who your brand's audience is.

Step 3: Establish a mission statement for your brand.

Step 4: Do research on brands in the same industry as your business.

Step 5: Outline the differentiating benefits and qualities offered by your brand compared to competitors.

Step 6: Create a brand logo and tagline.

Step 7: Form a brand voice to communicate with customers.

Step 8: Create a brand message and pitch.

Step 9: Find ways to demonstrate your brand's personality.

Step 10: Implement brand integration into your business in every way possible.

Once you have implemented branding successfully, you can start marketing your brand in various ways.

# Chapter 2: Aligning Branding With Your Business Goals

# Chapter 2: Aligning Branding With Your Business Goals

Branding is not merely about designing a logo and brand name. Your brand has to influence customers in a way that they want to buy your products or pay for your services. You have to align your business objectives with branding. Regardless of what your business is, marketing and branding will play an essential role in achieving your business goals. They are related to boosting sales, gaining a larger audience for your brand, increasing brand awareness, and even delivering better customer care. All of these can be achieved by aligning business goals with branding. The role of aligning marketing strategy in attaining these objectives is crucial. Branding and marketing will not be sufficient by merely aiming to fulfill the objectives set for your business. The best results will be obtained by effectively aligning the goals and the branding strategy at the same time.

## 2.1 Why Must Business Goals Align With Branding?

It is crucial for you to understand that your business goals should align with branding. Remember that the two are not mutually exclusive. If you want a proven implementation of your business goals, internal alignment is essential.

Businesses can establish specific and attainable goals if they take the marketing input into account at every level. A clear and realistic plan can then be formulated to achieve business goals within a particular time frame.

Brand strategy should include a defined process that will help to use the right resources and to achieve the set goals. The alignment of these two elements will help in this.

You will receive clear progress reports at every stage of the process. The measurement tools can be used to attain all the relevant metrics. It will help to identify any requirements for adjustments in your business plan.

**2.2 How to Align Branding With Business Goals**

### Use branding and marketing for goal setting

The insights from marketing will help you identify opportunities for and threats to your business. Use the insights to be specific about the goals set for your brand. Instead of a generic goal, like increased revenue, determine how you can do this. The data from marketing and branding will help you identify what you need to work on. Identifying such clear goals will, in turn, help you create a more effective branding strategy.

### Use the data to set informed objectives from your marketing strategy

It is essential to set goals that are realistic and achievable. Setting specific goals after data analysis will help in this. Focus on getting details from the marketing data that will help to set business goals in a clear way for the entire organization.

### An agile marketing culture should be nurtured

If every team has a marketing-oriented focus in an organization, their marketing strategy can be even more effective and result in attaining all the set business goals. Foster a culture where everyone in your organization feels responsible for delivering high-quality products to consumers via your brand.

## *Marketing goals should be adjusted according to circumstances*

Things may not always go to plan, and your goals should also be adjusted accordingly. Aligning business goals with marketing will help to ensure the achievement of larger goals even while adjusting smaller milestones.

**Your Quick Start Action Step:**

Refer to section 'How To Align Branding With Business Goals' where the steps for aligning your business goals with branding are mentioned. Following these steps to help you fulfill the objective of this chapter.

# Chapter 3: Finding and Serving Your Target Customers

# Chapter 3: Finding and Serving Your Target Customers

## 3.1 Target Audience

Simply put, target customers are a group of people who are more likely to respond positively to your brand products, services, or promotions. Before you start any branding or marketing campaign and move ahead with social media marketing, you have to understand your target customers. In this chapter, we will focus on learning how to target the right audience for your brand. The right audience may differ according to what your business provides. If your company offers sports equipment, your target audience is people who play those sports. If your brand offers clothes for men, your target audience is the male gender. In this way, the audience for a brand can be limited or vast depending on the variety of products or services you provide. Your marketing strategies thus need to be oriented towards the target audience for your brand. Target audiences have to be analyzed based on factors such as their age, gender, income, etc.

## 3.2 Importance of Finding the Target Customers for Your Brand

A target audience is essential because the channel, language, or platform that you use to communicate with specific audiences will not always be effective with others. Your team needs to identify a target audience for your brand to market your brand effectively to them, and this will help you find the tone that is required to reach out to specific customers. A target audience analysis will provide direction for your marketing campaign and help you build relationships with the right people.

It is all about relevancy while designing a profile for your target audience. The products and services your brand offers should match the audience you are marketing to. This is when they will convert to real sales. It is hard to resonate with a vast audience because people are looking for different things and one campaign cannot provide it all. For a deeper connection with customers, you need to identify who the real customers are as well as their needs and interests.

## 3.3 How to Find Your Customers?

In this economy, it is vital to identify the target market. It is exceedingly expensive to target everyone without a clear audience. If you target a niche audience, it will help you compete with the most significant brands from your industry as well. A generalized target can be a disadvantage for your business. It's not just about getting any customer possible to be interested in your brand. Your marketing strategy will fare better if you know the exact customer base that is more likely to drive sales for you. Identifying them and customizing a campaign with them in mind will be ten times more effective. Don't fear excluding other potential customers just because you are targeting a few. The point is that a particular target audience will help you spend money in a better way and assure you of good returns which can be re-invested in marketing for others later. A clear defined audience will make it easier for you to determine the places and people you need to market to.

1. First, you need to look at the current customer base you have. Pay attention to these people who already buy from your brand and notice which products or services the majority opt for. Find out about these people, and you will find that others like them are potential customers for your brand.

2. Look into your competition or others in the same business. See who these brands are targeting and who their customers are. You don't have to chase and try to turn those customers towards your brand. Try to find a niche market that your competitors are missing out on and target them.

3. Analyze the products and services your brand offers. Make a list of all that your business offers.

4. Choose specific demographics you want to target. You need to figure out who needs and is more likely to purchase your product or service — factors like age, location, gender, income, occupation, and education matter here.

5. You also need to consider psychographics like personality, values, lifestyle, behavior, and attitude of these potential customers.

6. After deciding on a target market, ensure you have considered the following: Are you targeting enough people, and will these people benefit from your product? What is their probable income and will they be able to afford your products? Are these people accessible and will you be able to connect with them?

Don't worry too much about the target breakdown. You can always target multiple audience groups. It helps you to start with a smaller, more focused audience, as it will guide you in creating the right kind of branding campaign and promotions. If you make a little effort, you can find out a lot about your customers and create an effective target audience list for your brand. As your brand grows, so will your audience.

**Your Quick Start Action Step:**

Step 1: You need to set a schedule to apply the steps that are outlined in the previous section.

Step 2: Set aside time to learn more about your customers and to master your brand. You cannot sell your brand to others until you know what and how you are selling it.

Step 3: Take time to put yourself in the shoes of your potential customers. Empathize with them when you communicate with them as well.

Step 4: Study your customers and analyze them. Create content based on what would appeal to these customers.

Step 5: Be innovative and make changes in your product or service according to the needs of your consumers.

Step 6: Remember to stay honest with your target audience and don't try to hard sell with vague statements.

# Chapter 4: The One Critical Element in your Branding

# Chapter 4: The One Critical Element in your Branding

## 4.1 The Impact of Storytelling

Tales have been narrated since time immemorial, and the impact of stories remains the same until today. People have always been fascinated with stories and will remember a well-told story far longer than any facts. Storytelling can thus be used as a means to connect your consumers with your brand. Potential consumers who were introduced to a new brand via narration[7] and other means showed different results — those who were introduced via storytelling connected with the brand more and were more likely to become customers.

Fewer people were willing to be customers from the second group, and their outlook was not as

---

[7] How to Leverage Storytelling to Increase Your Conversions. (2019). Retrieved from https://neilpatel.com/blog/how-to-leverage-storytelling-to-increase-your-conversions/

positive as the first group. This demonstrates how a brand story can reinforce a positive association with your brand. Seeing this, a lot of brands have started using storytelling to connect with their target audience. This method has become even more relevant in recent times because consumers are looking for authenticity and more emotion from the brands they endorse. People don't want to buy things blindly anymore. They would rather be loyal to a brand they believe in and connect with. This is why storytelling is vital in establishing an emotional connection with people. It is most impactful when the content has an authentic voice, narrative and has relatable subject matter.

Use your brand story to defend your values and display excellence at all times. Don't use this storytelling medium to talk about yourself if you want it to work. It should not be a singular narrative about the brand and why consumers should buy your products. Instead, tell a story that indirectly but effectively fulfills this purpose while delivering something entertaining and touching to consumers.

## 4.2 The Importance of Creating a Story Brand

Creating a story brand will enhance the brand in a way that more people gravitate towards it.

No matter how things change and the world evolves in terms of technology and other advancements, some things will always remain the same. People will always move with emotion. Regardless of how effective your platform is in delivering content, the content itself needs to be moving. People are still interested in great stories that remind them of their humanity. A good marketing professional will know that a great narrative can be a useful tool in marketing. Creating a brand story will bolster connections with your target audience.

Creating a compelling story will evoke interest in your brand, but it is not enough. You have to improve discoverability by creating non-linear content that is not the same as unilateral storytelling. Your target audience will be engaged further if you create personalized experiences.

## 4.3 How to Make a Story Brand

By now, you might be trying to figure out how you can create a story brand. Your brand story should move your audience effectively, and there are various examples of this displayed by other brands.

1. To create a memorable story about your brand, consumers need to be shown not just told. Weave a story in a way that you can naturally convey how great your brand is.

2. Create stories that inspire your target audience. It should be a story that makes them want to get involved with your brand and also feel like it will make a difference in their lives. You can tell stories that may not be related to your brand; however, mention your product without being too obvious. This kind of storytelling campaign should be interesting without being hard-selling.

3. People should be able to identify with your brand. When you tell a story,

include characters that your target audience will identify with. This will help them relate to your brand and feel compelled to become your customer.

Your story should highlight the positives in your brand and product without being too obvious. The main point behind being a storytelling brand is to market it to people via the story. Create a story that tells the narrative in a way that manages to convey the benefits of your brand to your consumers.

**Your Quick Start Action Step:**

Schedule time to carry out the steps above and think about what story to share.

1. Create a character that your target audience will identify with and root for. This character should embody your brand ideals.

2. Integrate brand values into the content.

3. Make use of the timeline feature on Facebook or social media platform of choice and display how your company

began and reached its current status.

4. Create content, like videos, which highlight what happens behind the scenes at your company. Increase the human element of your brand and display it to the public. Share personal stories about the people who work for your organization.

5. Use your origins as a means for storytelling, including your brand. Your humble beginnings will appeal to people and make them want to believe in you.

6. Be honest with your consumers about your brand. Be consistent, persistent, and exercise restraint when it is called for.

7. Dissect tales that are brilliant and effective even when they are simple.

# Chapter 5: Integrating Branding into Content

# Chapter 5: Integrating Branding into Content

## 5.1 Content for Branding

In this chapter, you will find out more about the importance of content and how you can integrate branding into the content used by your business. This will include blogs, videos, podcasts, etc.

The preferences of the current generation have resulted in a lot of changes in the world of marketing. Your business cannot target millennials in traditional ways. They prefer a more meaningful connection with brands, and this can be attained with the help of branded content. These days people can easily block ads with the help of various apps or ad blockers. So if you want your content to grab their attention, instead of being blocked, you need to create great branded content. There are differences between older advertising and branded content that you need to understand.

There are higher chances of sales from brands

that create custom content; therefore, the concept of branded content emerged. This term is relatively new in the marketing world and should not be confused with native advertising. Native advertising is using paid ads that complement the feel, look, and function of the social media platform it uses. The market is quite saturated and branded content will help you deal with this issue by surpassing the performance of traditional advertising.

## 5.2 Integrating branding into business content

Integrating branding into business content is essential because:

- Branded content is more effective, causing traditional methods of product pushing to become entirely obsolete. There are many newer ways to push content, such as sponsored posts on your feed or marketing emails.

- People won't go around looking for marketing content proactively. However, they will do so when you provide branded content that they relate to. A video telling a story about people who use products from your brand can be one of the top searched videos on YouTube within a week. A branded content campaign will get a lot of recognition from people in the right way if you deliver it appropriately.

- It is not just about getting more customers and generating sales. Branded content helps to strengthen the brand's relationship with its audience.

- Branded content that does not revolve solely around the product is more attractive to customers. There are higher chances of this converting to sales than a blatant ad about your product.

## 5.3 How to Integrate the Brand into Content

Brand integration into content can be done in many ways.

You need to find a way to integrate your brand

organically with content. The integration should be done in a way that is relevant to consumers and the content at the same time. Brands should not just be seen as sponsors for content and instead be seen as a part of the content. For example, when you have a storytelling video being created, the brand should be included in it like a character. It should play a significant role in the content so that people take notice of it.

Think about a TV show or movie that fits with the image of your brand. Choose productions that have already shown effectiveness in brand integration and generated results. For instance, make sure that your brand icon is extremely visible, and the duration of the visual is long enough to be effective. Also, make sure that your product is not just kept passively but that a character uses it or touches it. Try to get the main character of the show or movie to use the brand product. Also, insert actual advertisements about the same product during infomercials. This will make the audience take notice of it and remember it later. Ideally, this would happen over time, not merely during one episode, if you want it to be effective.

**Your Quick Start Action Step:**

To learn more about content and content marketing and how it can help your business, check out **"Content Marketing: Proven Strategies to Attract an Engaged Audience Online with Great Content and Social Media to Win More Customers, Build your Brand and Boost your Business"** by Gavin Turner.

# Chapter 6: Leveraging Social Media Marketing to Help Build your Brand

# Chapter 6: Leveraging Social Media Marketing to Help Build your Brand

## 6.1 How Can Social Media Marketing Build Your Brand?

Social media marketing involves Internet marketing on social media networks by sharing various types of content with potential customers. The fact is, social media marketing can be a powerful tool for any business. It does not matter if your business is small scale or large scale; social media will help you reach prospects or customers from all over the world. You can bet that your customers are active on some form of social media, and if your brand does not have a presence there, you are missing out. There are great social media platforms like Facebook, Instagram, Twitter, Pinterest, etc. which can be used to interact with a broad audience. If you use the correct strategy, you can use social media marketing to bring remarkable growth for your brand. It will help to drive sales and also create a devoted following for your brand over the years. SMM involves posting varied text content, images, videos, etc. that will help to drive the audience towards your business. These platforms are usually free for use, and this makes it a definite bonus. Most of them also offer paid advertising, which you can use for the benefit of your brand.

Social media marketing will help you achieve several goals:

- It will promote the name of your brand or business
- It will help you increase traffic on your website
- It will help to build conversions
- It will raise awareness about your brand
- It will help you in creating a brand identity as well as positive brand association
- It provides a medium for communicating and interacting with your target

audience.

## 6.2 Why Is Social Media Helpful?

If you are still standing on the sidelines when it comes to social media marketing, this is the best time to get on the bandwagon.

The following are just some of the reasons why social media marketing is the right choice for your brand:

### *Exposure*

The most significant advantage of social media is that it will get the word out about your brand to a lot of people in a short amount of time. It gives you extensive exposure and also provides you an opportunity to establish a relationship with your target customers. The people who follow you on social media will help to spread the word about your brand to even more people via their profiles.

### *Global Reach*

Social media is extremely popular all over the

world right now. At least 70% of[8] the population across the globe is currently active on some form of social media or the other. This means that the likelihood of most of your customers being on social media is quite high. Creating a page for your brand on some social media sites will get you off to a great start even as a small business. Social media has an extensive reach, and with its dynamic functionality, your business will benefit from a presence on such platforms.

**Pocket-friendly**

Another great advantage is that social media marketing is extremely cost-effective. You should take advantage of the advertising features offered by these platforms since they are quite affordable compared to others. Use such adverts to promote offers, new products, or any content. Traditional advertising can be costly compared to social media advertising. However, you will be reaching a lot more people at a much smaller price. Cost-effectiveness is

---

[8] Topic: Social Media Statistics. (2019). Retrieved from https://www.statista.com/topics/1164/social-networks/

important because you get higher returns with low investments and also have sufficient money to invest in other business expenses.

## *Wider audience*

It also defies age barriers since social media can reach people of all ages or demographics. The significant range of people registered on social media can be anywhere from 18 to 65, and these are all potential customers for your business. So it doesn't matter what the target audience of your brand is, social media will help you reach out to all of them.

## *Communication with the audience*

Social media marketing also gives you a medium to really connect with your audience. It encourages two-way communications where your customers or potential leads can act directly and ask questions or make inquiries about your products. You can also use social media to get direct feedback from customers and use this to resolve any issues. People are much more willing to communicate on social media than through random surveys or cold calls. Communicating with your customers will establish a relationship that they will appreciate. Social media will also allow you to learn more about your customer's interests and what you can do to attract them towards your brand.

## 24/7 coverage

People on social media are active. The average individual checks their social media profile at least 15 times a day. This gives you a chance to promote your brand consistently. In person, they might come to your store once or twice in a month. However, through social media, you can keep displaying your products and services to them.

## Deep connection

Social media allows you to share detailed information with your customers. You can keep updating them about your brand in terms of events, products, etc. Consumers prefer using social media to learn about brands compared to any other medium. As long as your profiles are public, you have high chances of appearing on your consumer's search lists.

### *Email marketing*

It also makes a significant impact when it comes to email marketing. You can use social networks to share your email newsletters. This spreads your content further and generates buzz about your brand. Social media sites can be used to get more people to sign up for your mailing list.

### *Loyal customer base*

It gives you the opportunity to gain a loyal customer following. This is one of the major agendas of social media marketing. The better you connect with your audience, the more your customers are satisfied and likely to stay loyal to your brand. Regular interaction shows your customers that you care about their needs and opinions. This creates a positive impression, and they return the favor by spreading the word about your brand to others. Satisfying some customers will help you gain more, just by word of mouth.

### *Greater conversion*

The conversion rate on social media is the percentage of users who end up using your service or buy your product through your social media page. The conversion rates for social media marketing are high. The more the visibility for your brand, the better your chance at conversions. The activity on your social media platforms will lead to more viewers and traffic. The humanization factor of social media marketing gives your brand a positive look. Sales and brand presence will increase when you take the time to develop good relationships with customers. If you leave a good impression on viewers via social media, they will be more likely to remember your brand when they need a product or service that you provide.

Social media is present across the world. Most of these primary social media services are available via mobile apps, and this makes it very easy for people to access them regardless of where they are in the world. All they need is an Internet connection. This is a significant benefit for small businesses in particular. A presence on social media will improve their chances of being discovered by potential customers. People don't just use social media to talk to each other anymore. They use them to look for products, services, and brands, which will appeal to them and improve their quality of life. It also helps you to target people according to geographical locations if your business is local. Various social media sites allow you to send messages and target geographic audiences while marketing.

So stop sitting on the sidelines and start utilizing the benefits of social media marketing for your brand.

## 6.3 Building Your Brand Using Social Media Marketing

The following are general guidelines for building your brand using social media marketing.

### *Social media marketing strategy*

Most people waste a lot of time merely building a product and not enough time making a marketing strategy and testing it to see if it is going to work. Just as you need to find a niche, product, and an audience for your business, you also need to build your social media marketing strategy. You may be someone who decided to join various social media platforms, created a great page with information on the service and product before launching your product without a strategy, because you wasted too much time focusing on the product. Your page will soon be a barren land without a social media marketing strategy. Just like how you asked yourself some questions before building up a business, it is essential to ask a few questions regarding marketing. For example, what is your goal? Are you using social media to gain likes and follows? Why do you need likes and followers? Is it so you can create a new source of sales? Who is your targeted audience? What are your tactics? Who are your teammates? How are they helping you in your social media marketing? All these questions are crucial for setting up a social media marketing strategy. You need to have a set goal. You need to make plans and take steps to attain that goal, as well as set time limits to check on yourself, to ensure you are not wasting your time.

### *Know your target audience*

Not knowing your audience is a big fail for any business. A target audience is the most important of all. You may be working hard in a business, but if you are unaware of who your audience is, then you will end up nowhere.

### *Link to other social media platforms*

Social media marketing works best when linked with other profiles, not only should accounts be linked together on different social media platforms, but they should also be directly connected to websites, email, contact info, and address details. Not connecting any accounts is like leaving this social media account as an island; it reduces the amount of reach to a particular audience as well.

### *Use images*

With the advancement in social media marketing, there has been a rise of photographers who take professional shots of various business products and services to tell the audience of their services. Social media business accounts should include images to draw attention and convey to consumers their products and services.

## Use hashtags

Hashtags get used on different social media platforms to boost views and are inserted in various trending topics too. For businesses, it is suggested to use hashtags to double engagement. Using strategically chosen hashtags can help companies find their target audience as well as help with their brand's influence.

## Create a positive environment

Insulting brands and getting into arguments in the comment section will create a backlash. Whenever a negative comment pops up, brands reply, giving lame excuses, apologizing, or straight out ignoring. Social media offers a great chance to connect with the customers, so it is an excellent opportunity to reach out to the customers and make improvements from the feedback instead. Negative comments are just honest opinions given by the user regarding the product. The more detailed the feedback, the more you will understand the shortcomings of your product. When you face negative feedback, engage with the customer as soon as possible, and assure them that the product quality will be better next time. Make it a rule to never engage in personal attacks.

### Interact with followers on social media

Social media is meant to be an interactive platform, and consumers always expect responses from businesses on social media. Responding to their inquiries, thanking them, and addressing their complaints helps consumers feel connected to the brand. Companies should set strategies to respond to the customers because it helps build trust between the brand and consumer, which will affect future sales and also creates opportunities for word of mouth marketing.

### Create an easy browsing experience

The business should make its customers feel at ease while shopping from their page. An easy to navigate browser is always going to be a better shopping experience for customers, rather than complicated double-clicks on so many links and different product pages. The business should link directly to product pages instead of boring home pages.

### *Include product details*

Descriptions are a crucial part of a business in the social media sector, and marketing without describing the item is a failure. When selling products on a social media platform, it is essential to be as descriptive as possible. Include price, material details (if it is a cloth-related market), color availability, as well as size details. Missing these points could create confusion for your probable consumer.

### *Post differently on different social media platforms*

Every platform in social media is distinct in its own way; your marketing skills should be as well. Avoid treating every social channel in the same way. Try and plan a time to determine content and engagement levels for each of the social channels and develop accordingly. There are high chances of your social accounts growing stale if you keep posting the same thing everywhere.

## *Avoid posting unrelated topics*

Be strategic when it comes to social content. There needs to be a thought process behind every post. If your business randomly posts unrelated topics on their social media to engage the audience, then it will only work if your luck is good. Every social media platform is different, so your social strategy should have a thought process behind it.

## *Spambots*

Some businesses buy followers to present themselves better. This usually happens when there is little interaction with customers. A page that is loaded with information but no real followers weakens social presence. To avoid these mistakes, it is essential to have patience and build a slow but genuine follower base.

## *Be dedicated to the platform*

As far as social media marketing is considered, consistency is vital. Creating a social media page on your business and forgetting to post will affect your brand's growth. Keeping an updated page will help consumers interact more and help build a relationship with the customers.

## Include varied types of content

Most businesses make a mistake of posting the same content, making it always self-promotional or self-centered posts that are only about the business can bore followers and decrease engagement. It is vital to keep your followers entertained while social media marketing. Include personal blogs in your posts, as well as videos and share customer reviews, include high-quality images and don't ignore festivities, make sure to wish everyone well for every festival. Don't make your social media platform a boring one revolving around just one topic.

## Avoid low-value content

Posting content regularly will boost your views and chances of engagement but do not post just for the sake of posting. This is when most businesses start posting low-value content. It is one of the biggest mistakes social media marketers make. Do not post content unless it gives value and is attention-worthy, or else the consumers will ignore it.

## *Take advantage of metrics provided by some social media platforms*

Use analytics to track and analyze the shares and traffic visiting your site. Track your performance on social media; there's no point in using social media for business if you are not aware of the insights. Measure the popularity and quality of your posts and your followers. By keeping a track on the engagement factors and demographic filters, it gets easier for the software to differentiate what is useful for your marketing campaign.

## *Stay updated with trends and check on any drops in engagement*

Monitoring customer engagement and the trends in the social media platform will help you understand if buyers are getting what they want, if they are happy with the product, and will help you determine what they truly want.

## Don't spread yourself thin on every social media platform

Unless you have a strong team to manage each page, you won't be able to handle all the social media marketing while running a business of your own. So dedicate your time on just one or two of the social media platforms and boost followers since it will get easier to get better responses from followers. The key to successful social media marketing is to give enough time to a platform for it to grow. So start slow, build a genuine follower-base in an account with valuable content, instead of jumping into many platforms all at the same time and failing in all of them

## Set up a team

Some people are born to be social media marketers; they have a different way of presenting their social media presence, while some may have to work harder to get their social media game on. That is why setting up a team is very important. This team should include an analyst, product expert, communicator (one who is directly available to the consumers) and a coordinator who will help all three. Select a team who has experience managing social media and blogs and are good at it; they will be able to handle any negative and positive issues comfortably.

## *Social media policy*

This is important, as most companies skip this part. Having a social media policy will save a company's reputation and instructs employees on issues like not posting complaints about customers, or not posting confidential information about the company. This helps the employee understand that what they say and do online can negatively affect the company's name. Having a social media policy will help avoid a public relations disaster and will protect the company's overall image.

## *Do not use too many automated link posting*

While using automated link posting does help

ease the load of manual efforts, it can give viewers an impression of a bot. Marketers should avoid using this if they do not want to seem like a spamming site. Automation can be useful for occasionally reposting content, but it can be overwhelming if you keep posting the same content, so it is important to understand when to automate and when to upload manually.

## *Market on the right sites*

Different social media marketing has a diverse audience, and some marketers fail to understand that. The first step is to identify your target audience, their age group, and any other pertinent details you can think of. Facebook is a social media page with more or less every age group active, while Instagram is a platform with mostly 18 to 29 year-olds active and only 18 percent of middle-aged users. Twitter is another social media with the same demographics as Instagram but a slightly higher percent of middle-aged users. Pinterest is a platform where the age groups of 18 to 49 are active equally, with 45 percent of the active members being women. Linkedin is a professional platform with 31% of men participating in this platform and 50 percent of those being college grads.

## [9]*Reviews matter*

Reviews are everything for a business, and they matter a lot because 90% of consumers read customer reviews before considering to visit a business site or purchasing any product online. 88% of all consumers trust the reviews as much as they would trust a personal recommendation. 72% of consumers have said that positive reviews make them trust the business more. 10% of all website traffic value is credited to online reviews, and 90% of customers purchase a product after seeing an online review[10].

---

[9] Social Media Use 2018: Demographics and Statistics. (2019). Retrieved from https://www.pewinternet.org/2018/03/01/social-media-use-in-2018/

[10] Anderson, M. (2019). 88% Of Consumers Trust Online Reviews As Much As Personal Recommendations - Search Engine Land. Retrieved from https://searchengineland.com/88-consumers-trust-online-reviews-much-personal-recommendations-195803

Reviews also help list your business in Google's knowledge panel when someone searches for your company, so it is beneficial to maintain a good rating.

# Chapter 7: Promoting Your Brand with Facebook

# Chapter 7: Promoting Your Brand with Facebook

## 7.1 About Facebook

Most people are already familiar with Facebook, but for those who are not, we will provide a short introduction. Facebook, Inc. is one of the most popular social networking sites in the world. Based in California, this site was founded by Mark Zuckerberg, Eduardo Saverin, Andrew McCollum, Dustin Moskovitz, and Chris Hughes while they were in college at Harvard. The site grew drastically from its beginning in 2004 and is now prominent among the biggest companies in the world, such as Apple. It also acquired Instagram and Whatsapp in the recent past. The website has more than 2 billion users who are active, and these are all potential customers for your business. This is why you need to get started on building a Facebook page for your brand and promote it as much as possible. The website is free for use and profiles can be created for personal or business use. You can use this page for posting photos, multimedia, messages, promotions, offers, etc.

Creating a Facebook business page would be an excellent way for your brand to offer promotions and interact with consumers. It has many features that can be used for promoting your brand. Make sure to fill in all the details on the Facebook page so that consumers get sufficient information about your brand. Also, add all of your contact information so that they know how to connect with you. You can add phone numbers, email addresses, office locations, and business hours. You need to make use of the space available on the page and enter complete information. Engage with the people who follow your page and interact with them as often as possible.

## 7.2 How to Create a Facebook Ad

Follow these steps to create a Facebook ad for your brand.

1. First, go to Facebook.com/advertising or log in to your Facebook page
2. Click on "Manage your Ads"or "Settings"

3. Click on "Create Ad"

4. Then select "Page Likes" under "What kind of results do you want for your ad"

5. Enter a URL under the blank space given under "Page Likes"

6. You can select up to six different images on this page for six different ads

7. Under "Edit Texts and Links" fill out your headline

8. Then you fill out your ad information under "Texts"

9. Tick on sponsor stories: here you can help people discover your business through their friends

10. You can choose "News Feed" or the "Right Column"

11. Next, create your audience by filling out location, age group of the targeted audience, gender, interest (business industry, etc.), connection (different social platforms), relationship status,

and education

12. Enter your Campaign name

13. Select your budget per day

14. Schedule your start date and end date

15. Click on "place order."

16. Now your Facebook advertisement is ready

## 7.3 How to Promote Your Brand on Facebook

Facebook is a great medium to promote your brand, even if it is just starting. Being on Facebook is beneficial to businesses, as it has many tools that can be useful in generating new customers and then sales.

### *Create a business page*

Create a Facebook business page for your brand. A business page is unlike a personal profile where people have to friend you. In this brand page, people have to like your page to view its content. Customize the page according to your brand image. Use the logo and tagline prominently. Add information like location, business hours, website details, etc. on it.

### Regular meaty posts

Post regularly but makes sure the content is excellent. Share updates about your brand and offer exclusive promotions to people who like your Facebook page. Share photos and videos about your brand and the products it offers. Facebook insights will help you analyze how your posts are working.

### Use other social media channels to link account

After the page is created, you need to share the page with people via other mediums. Also, send invites to your current customers. Add a link to your Facebook profile on your main website as well. Direct traffic here and vice versa from other social media profiles.

### Interact with the audience

Engage your Facebook followers via posts. Interact with them and respond to any questions or concerns they may have. Create a personal connection and be accessible. Leverage potential customers via their current customer base. Engaging with your followers will help others view the content as well. Also, hold contests to gain new followers by offering a prize as an incentive.

### Facebook Ads

Use Facebook ads to reach out to a targeted audience effectively. This tool has been handy for other brands, and you should use it for promoting your brand as well.

### Your Quick Start Action Step:

Step 1: Set a schedule to apply steps in '*How To Promote Your Brand On Facebook*' section

Step 2: Take time out to create the completed Facebook profile first.

Step 3: Invite people to like the page and follow your brand on Facebook.

Step 4: Keep updating content regularly. Create content when you can and set a schedule to upload them once in a while. Don't upload too much at once like spam.

Step 5: Promote any new products and services and connect with your customers as often as possible.

Step 6: Use Facebook Analytics to analyze your brand page.

# Chapter 8: Promoting Your Brand with Instagram

# Chapter 8: Promoting Your Brand with Instagram

## 8.1 About Instagram

Instagram is probably one of the most widely used social media platforms at this moment. It is a service that allows all its users to share photos and videos on its platform. Currently, this business is now owned by Facebook, Inc. The Instagram application was launched in 2010 exclusively for iOS devices but is now available for Android and Windows devices as well. You can upload any image or video on Instagram and then use various filters and photo editing tools to improve them further. Your account can be kept private and accessible only to followers you permit. However, as a business, you will probably have to opt for a public profile that any Instagram user will be able to view. Hashtags and locations allow you to search for particular types of content on Instagram. There is an Explore page that displays various trending content according to your viewing history. Users are permitted to like and comment on any photos or videos that another user uploads. Instagram is one of the social media platforms that saw the fastest growth over a short period.

According to statistics, nearly a billion active users are registered on Instagram as of 2018.[11] The number is staggering and gives you an idea of why we recommend that you use this particular platform for marketing. Think of the millions of possible customers you can gain just from this particular platform. Instagram is not just about people sharing their photos with friends and family. It has gradually become one of the most lucrative platforms for businesses across the world. Search for any famous brand, and you will find their page on Instagram. The best marketing teams have recognized and utilized the potential of Instagram as a business tool over the past few years. There are thousands of individuals who have emerged as

---

[11] Instagram: active users 2018 | Statista. (2019). Retrieved from https://www.statista.com/statistics/253577/number-of-monthly-active-instagram-users/

influencers and earn money through Instagram.

The large-scale brands that you should emulate have set up teams that regularly upload unique and exciting content to keep their customers engaged. Take a look at the feeds of some big brands and notice their following. This is what you should aim for as well. The majority of users on Instagram are willing shoppers. So if you want to sell your product or service, this is one of the easiest ways. You can do this without even trying giving out a sales pitch to clients. Just post the right kind of content on your Instagram feed, and your consumers will follow and engage with your brand. If you are an active user on Instagram, you can probably understand what we are saying and just how strong of a platform Instagram is. Even if you aren't familiar with it, we will help you understand why Instagram is useful for promoting any brand.

There are many ways in which Instagram features can help in the promotion of your brand:

**8.2 How to Create a Photo Ad on**

**Instagram**

Creating a photo ad on Instagram is easy and cost-effective with good returns. The following steps will guide you in creating one for your brand.

***Connect Instagram to the brand's Facebook page***

Step one is to ensure that your Instagram account is connected to the brand's Facebook page. If not, the ad cannot be created.

1. First, go to Facebook and click on Settings.

2. Then click on Instagram Ads and select Add an Account.

3. Assuming you already have an existing Instagram account, click on Add an Existing Account and enter the login details.

4. Then click on Confirm. Any ad that runs on Facebook can now be published on Instagram as well.

### *Select the ad type for your Instagram ad*

The possible objectives are clicks to website, mobile app installation, or video views. Select the image ads that will have a button to drive users to click. Then follow the next few steps:

1. Select the ad targeting options that will let you select location, interests, demographics, etc.

2. Use attention-grabbing images and avoid using any stock photos.

3. Leverage popular hashtags to direct more views.

## 8.3 How to Promote Your Brand on Instagram

### *Set up an optimized Instagram account for your business*

This is a business account and should not be treated as a personal one. You cannot share your vacation pictures and food posts on this account. The followers for this account are the targeted audience for your brand. So you need to post content that is relevant to your brand

and customers. If you have a website, Instagram allows you to add a direct link in your bio. You can use this feature as an opportunity to direct traffic to your site. Set the name of your brand as your Instagram username or select something as closely related as possible. Remember that the account should keep your brand name consistently recognizable. Even if someone randomly searches for your business on Instagram without knowing the exact username, they should be able to find your page. The bio should be short and attractive so that users get interested in your page. Also, keep it informative so that they get an idea about your brand. You can choose to give a concise description of your business in the bio section of your profile. Try to keep it light and look at the pages of other competitors to get an idea of what you should be doing. You don't have to worry about keywords here, so go with a simple but effective bio that tells people who you are and what you do. Add a dash of personality to your bio for added measure.

### *Create posts that your followers find*

*relevant*

Create posts that will make users want to follow your Instagram page. After you have done the basics of creating an Instagram profile and bio, you need to focus on your content. The photos and videos you post are crucial in determining whether Instagram will be a successful social media platform for you. This image-centric platform gives you an advantage over other social media. They say that a picture is worth a thousand words and you should use this to your advantage. Post the right kind of picture, and your audience will be hooked. They will follow you to keep track of more such content that they will expect from your business. Instagram is a visual world, and you need to post visually appealing content.

One thing to remember here is that you have to avoid hard-selling. Trying to sell something via Instagram is not the same as doing it in person. You don't have to have a pitch like a salesperson and convince the buyer that they should opt for your product or service. The photo or video you post should do all the talking. If your product looks great on the post, your work is done. Your audience will believe more of what they see and less of what they hear. So avoid a desperate sales pitch trying to convince people, wield your influence but don't be pushy.

The power of photos is immense in this world of Instagram. Don't skimp on getting professional and high-quality images taken for your Instagram feed. The better and more detailed the pictures, the more your customers will tend to believe you. It will also make your feed look much more appealing and attractive. Hire experts who will deliver great creative content for your Instagram feed so that your followers are hooked on it. Instagram will direct traffic that will turn into sales. Don't use Instagram as a photo sharing platform; look at it is a platform to connect to your prospective customers. A lot of users are on social media for guidance when choosing products, and your brand should not come off as too sales-driven. The impact of a beautiful and detailed photo will direct more sales towards your business than any product description or sales pitch. The images you upload should always reflect professionalism. Make sure that they are cropped the right way and avoid any blurry images.

Use photo-editing apps to enhance your images further. The in-app filters on Instagram itself will do most of the work for you. You have to make your photos stand out so that users don't just scroll past your photo. Also, remember to be a little consistent in the theme of your feed. We recommend keeping the pictures light and bright. These kinds of images generate more likes than any dark images.

If you look at individual business profiles, you will also notice that they like to stick to a particular color theme to make their Instagram feed look more aesthetically appealing, so try that trick for yourself too. Blue is more appealing to users than red. We also recommend that you upload pictures that tell the story of your brand. Users feel more connected with your brand when they see behind the scene images of any business. Share pictures of customers using your products too. Sharing this kind of lifestyle content generates more interaction from followers as opposed to other types of content. Display the culture and lifestyle associated with your brand so that you can connect emotionally with your consumers.

## What's in it for the followers?

Give users an incentive for following you on Instagram. Offer exclusive promotions that will only be visible on your Instagram page from time to time. When you offer discount codes or special announcements, people will want to be updated with your page. This makes them want to follow your page so that they don't miss out. Also, try giveaways once in a while because everyone loves a freebie. Various brands and influencers have been hosting giveaways on their Instagram page. These usually come with certain conditions like reposting a brand post and referring more followers. You can then hold a lucky draw and pull out a winner. Giving away a couple of free products is worth the extra potential customers you get. Users will also keep following you in hopes of winning another giveaway. Use eye-catching images and fonts when you announce sales or promotions. These will appeal to your followers and generate more views.

Exclusive announcements on your Instagram page will also allow your followers to plan and be ready to purchase any new products before others get to it. Various brands manage to sell out their products within the day just by using this trick. For instance, Kylie Jenner's makeup products are usually sold out as soon as her new stock is announced. This could be you if you plan your Instagram activity right. You can host events in various locations or at conventions and share these on Instagram. Using geotags will tell your followers where your event is being held, and you can invite them to come and participate. Insta-meets are a great way to interact with your followers and connect them with your brand.

## *Increase your Instagram following*

So now you know how to post the right kind of

content on your brand's Instagram page. You still need a strategy to get more followers on your page. For one, you can use hashtags to increase your brand's discoverability. Use popular tags that are related to your brand and the posts you create. When a user searches for that hashtag, your post will pop up. However, a lot of people tend to go overboard on hashtags. Just because you're allowed to use 30 hashtags does not mean you should use any random hashtags. Use hashtags that are relevant to your post. You can brainstorm and create hashtags specifically for your brand. Consumers can also use these hashtags when they upload pictures with your products or repost any of your content. This creates a community for your brand. Various data analysis apps will help you stay updated with the latest trending hashtags to use on your posts. Avoid using something too generic since your image will just be lost in the crowd. Try for more specific Hashtags that are relevant to your brand and your post. Instead of overpowering your caption with hashtags, add the hashtags in a comment after you post the picture. You can also create hashtags with your brand name or host an Insta-event. Create a contest where your followers post a picture while using your product. Add a suitable hashtag and ask them to share the image with that hashtag. You can also offer incentives for people with the most likes on their post. This creates a flow for your hashtag and makes it accessible while engaging your followers.

Another great tip is to create a team of Instagram ambassadors for your brand. These are the people who will post about your brand and share the benefits of using your product or service. This way, you get to reach out to more people. When other users praise and post about your brand, consumers are more likely to be convinced. Social media, as the name suggests, is all about being social. You do not have to refrain from posting and showing love to your fellow business competitors. If that is too much for you, then you can always share someone's work that you love, but don't forget to give them a shout out. This is a great way to make your page not only about you but other excellent content created by other people. This is also going to set a strong social media presence. You can also reward ambassadors by reposting their photos if they are of high quality and look good on your feed. When you share your users' content on your feed, it creates a positive connection with them that they genuinely appreciate and it will promote brand loyalty. Don't forget to tag the person whose post you are reposting.

## *Strengthen customer relationships by boosting engagement*

After creating great content and generating followers, you need to follow up. These followers can easily unfollow you and ignore your page or brand if you ignore them. Instagram allows for more engagement than Twitter. You can encourage communication between your brand and the consumers via Instagram. It enables you to get direct customer feedback and allows you to enhance your level of customer service. Use a call-to-action caption or ask a question when you post. Your captions should be active and inviting. For instance, you can ask a question about an image where the user can find the answer in the image itself. Your captions should not be too long. They have to be direct, short, and effective. Instagram content is one of the best ways to engage your followers. Contest posts see the most engagement since followers have something to gain from these. Select a prize that your followers will want to win and let them know what they will be winning by participating. Set rules where they have to follow your page and tag other friends in the comments. They can also repost the post with your contest hashtag for better chances of winning. However, refrain from hosting a contest until you have already built a somewhat active engagement among your followers. Also, try to reply to comments and direct messages from customers as much as possible. Your followers will always appreciate a response and attention. They will cease to engage in your posts if you don't engage with them directly from time to time.

**Measure your Instagram success over**

*time*

You have to persist in making an effort to keep your Instagram effective. You need to keep track of the growth happening through your Instagram. Use analytical tools to check which posts are compelling and which did not generate many likes or comments. This gives you insight into what your customers want and what you should be doing in the future. You cannot afford to be laid back and stop posting good content since this will cause users to unfollow your account. You can check the data to see which followers engage with your brand most often. Make them brand ambassadors and give them incentives to stay loyal to your brand.

Check the times at which your followers are most active and post during those periods. This will allow more of them to view your posts and generate more likes. An optimized posting schedule can be quite useful. Be consistent in how often you post as well. Try at least 3-5 posts every week. Avoid spamming and posting too much at once. A few good posts in a week will be enough. Instead of being online on Instagram all the time, use apps to schedule posts. This way, the posts can be created whenever you are free but be posted automatically on the optimized schedule. Your Instagram strategy should have realistic goals. Every follower will not always comment or like your posts. Only about 1 in 30 people might like your picture, and that's how it is for most brands. Try to increase this number over time as you measure your account growth and make sure the numbers don't fall.

**Your Quick Start Action Step:**
1. Set up an account for your brand on Instagram. Select a username related to your brand and upload a brand logo. Use a link to direct to your business website. Make the bio short and effective. This will barely take 5 minutes of your time if you have the right content ready.

2. Post an image that is high quality and is likely to attract users. Think from their perspective and look at competitors for reference. Add a witty caption that is

engaging. Make sure the image is high resolution. Offer promotions and announcements via posts once in a while.

3. Use relevant hashtags on your post and hire ambassadors to promote your brand.

4. Respond to any comments and messages from your followers.

5. Shout out to followers who post pictures with your products. You can do this via Instagram stories without having to add the images to your feed.

6. Use an app like Iconosquare to analyze how your posts are doing,

Instagram is a great tool to promote brand identity; make the most of it!

# Chapter 9: Promoting Your Brand with YouTube

# Chapter 9: Promoting Your Brand with YouTube

## 9.1 About Youtube

Creating a YouTube page for your brand is an excellent idea because videos can rank high in a very short amount of time. What most businesses do not know is that video marketing is growing and is getting bigger. 90% of consumers have admitted that a video of a product or service has played a significant role in their purchasing decision. Video marketing is already 80% of global Internet traffic and 85% in the United States[12]. Businesses have benefited because you do not have to waste a boatload of money on video making.

Most smartphones have great camera qualities, and most popular videos are straightforward, but with great sound and video quality, that is all it takes. It is vital to use the brand name in the URL extension of your page. After Google,

---

[12] The Importance of Video Marketing. (2019). Retrieved from https://digitalmarketinginstitute.com/blog/2018-04-25-the-importance-of-video-marketing

statistics say that YouTube is the next largest search engine. You have to make sure that your brand is easily found on both of these mediums. There are nearly a billion subscribers registered on YouTube, and people watch videos on this channel every single day. Instead of opting for TV advertisements, you can use YouTube videos, which will help you reach a majority of viewers between ages 18-50 years. The best thing is, this site isn't showing any signs of reduced growth rate and the number of viewers increases every single day.

**9.2 How to Create a Video Ad on Youtube**

The following steps will guide you in creating a successful YouTube ad for your brand. The things you need to get started are Google Ads account, YouTube account, and a Google analytics account. So you can create all of them under the same email address, and you are going to be able to link those accounts with Google.

1. The first step is to set up a Google ads account because YouTube ads are

managed through Google ads.

2. If you already don't have an existing Google ads account you can go to https://ads.Google.com/intl/en_IN/home/

3. Create a Google Ads account.

4. In addition to your Google Ads account, you should also have your own YouTube account.

5. Set up a Google analytics account. Google Analytics helps you track with conversion tracking.

6. Now that you have your YouTube account, Google Analytics account, and your Google account. You have to link those accounts, set up conversion tracking and you can import your conversion into Google, and so you can optimize for it. Go back to the Google ads account. Press the "Tool" icon. Go to "Linked Accounts" located under "Setup."

7. When you open a linked account, you will see a lot of options. Click on "Google Analytics" click "Details" and link your account.

8. If you are not familiar with how to link YouTube channels and Google ads: copy and paste this URL for details https://support.Google.com/Google-ads/answer/3063482?hl=en

9. How to link Google analytics and Google ads: https://support.Google.com/Google-ads/answer/1704341?hl=en&ref_topic=7548741. Links will allow those accounts to communicate with each other so you can have conversion backing set up in Google Analytics.

10. Go back to "Google Analytics" click on "Admin" to set up a goal. Add that goal into Google Ads and set up conversion tracking

11. To see conversion tracking, you can go to "Google Ads" under "Measurements"

click on "Conversion". There you will find whether it is recording conversions or there are no recent conversions.

12. You can see your conversion tracking is active by simply pressing on the "plus" (+) sign at the left-hand side of the conversion action page. This will allow you to add the conversion.

13. Click on "Campaign" and click on to "New Campaign"

14. There will be different options when you're creating a video campaign. You can only choose four options from the six. You can choose "Leads" for video campaigns to drive leads to your website, or "Website Traffic" for video campaign to drive website traffic, as well as leads or "Product and Brand Consideration" for video campaign to encourage people to explore your product and services, or "Brand Awareness and Reach" for video campaign to help you try and get your brand out there.

15. If you select "Brand Awareness and Reach" and click on "Video," you will get different types of options for the video ads. You can choose accordingly.

16. Under the "Brand Awareness and Reach" for video click on to "Continue" here you will see different bidding strategies.

17. You can do the same with the other three options then click "videos" to see the different bidding strategy.

18. Click on "Leads" go to "Video" click on "Continue"

19. You will be taken to a page where you have to fill the campaign name, budget, and dates. Here you can choose the start and end dates; you can set the delivery method as either standard or accelerated. If you choose 'standard", your budget will be spent evenly throughout the day, or choose "accelerated", and your budget will be spent as fast as possible.

20. Next is "Bidding": here you are telling

Google how much you want to pay for each conversion that you drive.

21. Select the languages your customers speak

22. Select the location where your target market is located

23. Next is "Content Exclusions": This step depends on your ads, and what you're advertising for and who you want to reach. Here you can find where your ad will be shown, for starters you can leave it as standard.

24. Go to "Excluded Content" here you can choose where you want your ads to be excluded from sensitive content.

25. Create an ad group name

26. Choose the demographics and targeted audience depending on the content you are trying to broadcast to the audience.

27. After you have done all the filling in the blanks according to what type of content

you are selling, you will come under a page to create a video ad. Upload your video to YouTube; you will see that box where the option to upload a video to YouTube is given.

28. Your video and should be at least 12 seconds.

    i. If your ad is 15 seconds or less you will be able to run as a non-skippable YouTube ad

    ii. Anything above 15 seconds is going to be a skippable YouTube ad

    iii. Your ad is generally not recommended to be above 3 minutes.

29. You can add any of your YouTube videos as an advertisement, but the longer ones will not make a good advertisement.

30. Copy the URL, which is at the top of the page, and paste the URL under the

"create your video ad" box.

31. Select "in-stream ad."

32. Click on "final URL": this is where you send your traffic. You can add any link where you want to direct your audience after your ad is shown.

33. Everything will be tracked into Google analytics because everything is linked together. You can go to "Acquisition" to see everything linked under Google Ads; here you can click on "video campaigns" to see the paid views, the cost per view users, and your conversions.

34. Name your ad

35. Save and continue to create your advertisement and view all the details of the ad you just created

36. Click on "Continue to Campaign."

37. If you want to keep testing different types of targeting, all you have to do is click the "plus sign" (+).

38. You will be taken to the group "Create your Ad Groups" to repeat the process.

## 9.3 How to Promote Your Brand on Youtube?

A good strategy will help you use YouTube to reach millions of people and improve your overall results from marketing. Let's look at how you can start promoting your brand on YouTube.

### *Create a strategy for YouTube promotion*

YouTube is a very time-consuming forum compared to other social media platforms. Creating videos requires more effort and time than posting images or tweets. To make the best of it, you need a proper strategy. Think of the goals you want to achieve from this site. For instance, do you want to use it for increasing brand awareness, more engagement, or for improving sales? In that case, identifying objectives will help you in creating the right content.

## *Think of the kind of videos you can create*

You don't have to worry about professional camera equipment if you are a small business and can't afford it. The quality of your content matters more. Create videos that will showcase your brand and its core values. Create how-to videos that will teach people how to utilize your products. You can also pay influencers to create videos for you to access their following. Also, make videos with famous personalities since viewers are always interested in such people and it will generate more views. You can also create a documentary video centering on your company. One thing to remember is that your content should not feature violence or other negativity. While some marketers may do this to get attention, this is always a big NO when it comes to social media marketing. Using foul language and other negativity, while maybe acceptable in our personal real-world life, is always best avoided in a social media page.

## *Manage your YouTube channel*

You need to manage your YouTube channel once you start posting videos on it. YouTube has fewer management tools compared with other social media platforms. You can use specific tools like Agorapulse to help you with this. It will help you to monitor and respond to all comments in one place. Common replies can be saved for comments as well. It will also help you to monitor any mention of your business on YouTube.

### *Use tools that will help you in creating better video content*

Video creation is much easier than before because there are a lot of tools to help you do this. Create animated videos, stop motion videos, and any video you want with these tools such as Wave and Slidely Promo.

### *Use search engine optimization*

If you want more people to find your videos, you need to optimize your content. Use keywords that represent your brand and keep the headline relevant to the content. Pay attention to the watch time because YouTube will promote videos that people watch more as opposed to ones they leave half-watched. Subscriber numbers will help you immensely since YouTube pushes channels that have a lot of subscribers.

***Tips:***

- Be as authentic in your content as possible.

- Create videos that will be useful for your audience and don't try to push your products too hard.

- Keep your videos short and exciting.

- Be consistent in uploading great videos so that your audience opts to subscribe to your channel.

- Find social media influencers to become brand ambassadors on YouTube for your brand.

- Create some videos with customer testimonials. This will appeal to loyal customers and help people connect with your brand.

**Your Quick Start Action Step:**

Start your YouTube promotion with the following steps:

Step 1: Create a channel with your brand logo and add a trailer video that introduces people to your brand. Keep it short and give YouTube users a reason to subscribe to your channel. Don't forget to use your logo as much as possible on your content.

Step 2: Create a great video that aligns with your brand campaign and upload it. Use hashtags that are popular and relevant. Also, share links to your video on other social media platforms. Get as many views on your video as possible. Also, have a branded hashtag that belongs to you. Encourage influencers to use this hashtag and promote your brand.

Step 3: Use the video description section to guide your followers. Tell them about the video and also add links to your brand website and other social media profiles. You can also add announcements and promotions on this section.

Step 4: Utilize Calls to Action on your videos. These encourage viewers to take action like leaving comments, liking or sharing the video, and subscribing to the channel.

Step 5: Use analytical tools to study which videos work and which don't benefit your brand.

# Chapter 10: Promoting Your Brand with Twitter

# Chapter 10: Promoting Your Brand with Twitter

## 10.1 About Twitter

Twitter is a social networking site where people communicate and share online news. It is also described as microblogging, as the messages allowed to be shared on this site are restricted to only 140 characters or less. This capped-messages format is what made Twitter so famous. Tweets are the short messages that people share on this site. The act of posting those short tweets is called Tweeting. People use Twitter through its website interface, and the registered users can retweet, post, and like other user's tweets. But unregistered users will only be allowed to read the tweets. Twitter is easy to use and can be downloaded for free and used through the app across devices. All you have to do is register your account for free and give yourself a Twitter name. Then you broadcast your tweets as frequently as you would like. You will build a following is no time. You can also follow interesting Twitter feeds, and you can always unfollow them when they start to get less appealing. Twitter has also been a great news-streaming place for people. When there are some natural calamities or other big news in some cities of the world, the microbloggers are all set out in a mission to share the news updates from around the world right from their phones. Like Facebook, you can use your Twitter page to display messages to visitors and also share links to your primary business site. The profile page provides an excellent space for marketing. You can create custom backgrounds with contact details, messages, and special promotions.

**10.2 Features to Promote Your Brand on Twitter**

*Create a specified bio*

The first thing that people look for is the bio of your page. That is the most important feature of Twitter to promote yourself. Use frequently searched keywords in your bio and add links to your business website for more details and your email address; this makes it easier for interested people to reach out. Create a clear bio of what your page means and attract the right audience.

## *Hashtags*

These popular search engines make it easier for the users to find the exciting content that they are looking for. You can use popular hashtags to connect with a large audience. You can also make your unique custom hashtags to promote your brand. The key is to use hashtags to make your feed pop up and allow users to discover your brand.

## *Use pictures and videos*

It is true that Tweets with pictures have more engagement than text tweets. A photo will say a lot more than the restricted characters of only 140; so post images relevant to your brand for more engagement and promotion of your brand. Twitter also allows 30 second long videos, which is another excellent way to promote a brand on Twitter.

## *Use Twitter's robust search tool*

By using Twitter's robust search tool, you don't have to wait for the audience and customers to come to you. This tool allows you to discover people who are interested in topics related to your brand. Use hashtags/common terms like "lid too tight" here people talk about their problems. You can solve their problem as a service to promote your brand.

### Create a Twitter contest

People are always after free stuff, so a giveaway contest is an excellent tactic for promoting your brand. Make a simple entry for this contest. Make it clear for the audience to know their eligibility to enter the contest; you can ask them to follow you to enter the contest or share the post you created. Be sure to follow the rules that Twitter has for brands. Choose a prize that is advantageous to your company, for example, a gift card to your brand, which they will use for your company. Here you can invite them to your page and make the most of serving the customers who may end up being a loyal customer after a pleasant experience.

### Promoted tweets for exposure

Use promoted tweets to get your tweets in front

of the targeted audience. To get your tweets promoted, you need to pay for promotion. It is worth the price as it gives you the ability to be discovered by the users who aren't following you and can improve the reach of the targeted audience. You can either create a post specifically for promotion or use one of your posts to promote your tweets; this helps give you more exposure. This also allows you to bring out the personality of your brand.

### *Twitter Ads*

Twitter ads are one of the most cost-efficient avenues as they are customizable, and you can decide how much you want to pay for the ad. Twitter ads are also very subtle, and they claim that their ads are the most memorable compared to other social media, as they don't regularly pop out like the rest of the ads on other sites. You can promote your entire account to be seen on the top of the list. Twitter ads are all about spreading awareness. You can promote certain products or launches.

### *Ad campaign*

Running a Twitter advertisement campaign is similar to running a Facebook advertisement campaign. An advertising campaign is linked to a single account, so it is essential to have a strong base of a dedicated business account. Click the Twitter ads page, and you will find a lot of options. You can choose according to your preference and pay accordingly. You can decide where you want your tweets to show up. The more places you try to promote your ads the, costlier your ad campaign will get.

### *360 degrees photos and videos*

This allows users to navigate 360 degrees of an image or a video. These are very popular, primarily when used for hidden clue-style content, where the users are expected to find a hidden prize in the 360-degree image or video. People love this, so they have great potential for more engagement.

### *Pin important tweets permanently*

Twitter allows you to highlight a particular tweet that can promote your post. Choose a tweet and pin it to your profile from the menu symbol located at the bottom right of the tweet. The tweet will remain on your profile until you remove it.

## Connect your Twitter to 'If This Then That' (IFTTT)

If This Then That is a free service where you can post automated repetitive tweets, posts, etc. This is especially useful if you have more than one Twitter account to handle. It saves a lot of time and helps you from missing out on related posts.

## Track tweets

You can track tweets by customizing your tweet alerts. There are hundreds of tweets made on an hourly basis, so this helps you avoid missing out on the important tweets. With the help of this feature, you will be notified when vital accounts tweet a post. This is important if you follow a particular brand competitor or some of the latest inspirational videos on Twitter marketing etc.

## Tweet archive

This feature helps you keep a record by documenting your activities; this also helps you look back on tweets you want to review. It is beneficial for business accounts to stay up to date with your work and track your time consumption and productivity on Twitter.

### *Share linked pages*

This is very important for business promotion; here, you can share your business websites to make it more convenient for respected customers.

### *Use power inbox*

This feature makes brands aware of the quality of the followers by giving a summary of the follower's biodata. It informs you about the follower's tweets, their followers and following, which helps your brand find the targeted audience. You can turn on and off the power inbox whenever you like.

### *Daily engagement*

Here you can engage with the people you are interested in. To interact with them, spend the first hours of the morning replying to these possible customers. Tweet at least three times per day and be consistent. It requires you to interact with others to build up loyal followers.

## The 80/20 rule

Use the 80/20 rule when tweeting, instead of posting all about your business, make sure that you provide 80% of value to your followers. Share a post of value that is positive and true. An interesting news article or fun facts related to your brand can boost your tweets and your brand. Use the remaining 20% to promote your business directly by sharing all about your business and company.

## Repost old tweets

There are a handful of followers who remember or check a post. So feel free to repost your past tweets and edit them if necessary. This way, there will be a lot of new followers who will see more of your content.

## Tweet chats

Tweet chats help you connect with a variety of

people. This puts you in direct contact with customers, brands, and influencers. It helps you to gain followers and promote your brand, to learn about your target audience and what they need, as well as identifying prospective influencers who could participate in your brand.

## 10.3 How to Create an Ad on Twitter

Twitter allows you to create ads, which can help your brand reach out to the millions of Twitter users active on their platform. Here are steps on how to create an ad on Twitter.

1. Log into your Twitter account - Click on the profile and settings icon located at the top right side of the page, and click on "Twitter Ads." After this, you will need to fill some required details, information like your country and time zone. After filling in the blanks press the "Let's Go" icon located at the end of the page.

2. After setting up the Twitter ads account - You can now create your first Twitter campaign. There are a few objectives you can choose from this page. You can

choose according to whatever your conversion goal is. For now, let's click on to "Website Click or Conversion". Here you can give your campaign a name, and you can also allow some budget to it.

3. Budget - Next select the "Advanced" icon, to choose to the pace of your campaign from standard or accelerated. The standard function allows you to divide your budget, and the accelerated function will exhaust your budget in no time.

4. Campaign Length - To choose the length of the ad campaign, choose the icon "When Do you Want your Campaign to Run" and choose either "start immediately", "run continuously" or "set start and end dates" according to your needs and budget.

5. Ad Group - Click on "next," and now you will enter the "ad group" page. Twitter follows the same method as other social media sites where your campaign can

have multiple ad groups. You can create the desired ad group by inserting a name on the "Ad Group Name" icon. You can also select a start and end time for the ad group. You can allot your budget under the budget options, which is optional because you have already allocated a budget for the ad campaign. Choose the "bid type" by clicking on the icon and choosing from three options: Automatic bid (Here the automatic bid of the campaign ad will be automatically added), Target cost (Here if you set an automated bid of two dollars, Twitter will make sure your average cost throughout the day for bidding is 2 dollars), or Maximum bid (If you set a maximum bid of 2 dollars then you will not be charged above 2 dollars for any click that you get on the ad).

6. Next steps - There are two additional options at the end of this page.

    a. Add an audience measurement

tag

    b. Add Double click tracking.

Both of these options require adding some code to your website. Adding code to your website helps with great design and improves the maintenance of your site. Click on next.

7. Creative page - You will be directed to a "Creative" page where you can finally select the tweets you want to promote. Here you can choose any tweets from your account to promote as an ad. Click on any of the tweets you would wish to promote. You can also decide where you want to show your ad to the viewers, on the right-hand side of this page you will see an option called "Ad Placement" here you can make that decision.

8. Select category - On the same "Ad Placement" option you can click on "Select Which Category Best Describes your Ad" to select a specific category for your ad. Click on the domain name and

then click on the "Next" icon at the top of the page.

9. Target page - The next page will lead you to the "Targeting" page here you will be able to find your audience. Select your preferred audience and fill in the demographics of your targeted audience. You can select the gender, age ranges, the location, language preferred, the technology used, the devices and platforms you are using whether it is a laptop, or a mobile phone device, Android or an iOS device. Select the icon according to what you prefer and use.

10. Choose the features - Click on audience features where you can choose the behavior, interest, and keywords to target. You can add keywords that describe the target audience and the kind of brand that you are. You can add additional options as keywords for your ad as this gives more exposure to your account. Click on "next."

11. Review - This is the final step where you will review the campaign that you created. You can make changes here if you want to edit any mistakes that you had made.

12. Final steps - Then click on "Launch Campaign." You will be directed to a payment method page to launch your campaign. Enter your card details and once this step is done, the ads will start to run.

That's it! Follow these simple steps, and you can create an attractive ad on Twitter for your brand.

## 10.4 How to Promote Your Brand on Twitter

Twitter is an excellent platform for promoting your brand due to the broad audience it provides you. Use the following tips to help you make the most of this.

### *Engage with influencers*

This is one of the fastest and easy ways to get

your brand promoted. You get an opportunity to gain more followers when you start engaging with an influencer; you will bring more traffic and more engagement to your account this way. An influencer already has a huge following and the audience that you want, so building friendship with an influencer can help your brand grow. You can use apps to find the top influencers and target audience. Check the followers for each influencer. Send them a tweet and get the relationship building.

### Use Twitter list

As the amount of people you follow on Twitter keeps expanding your timeline will be overwhelmed with so many tweets, which often will make you miss out on the essential tweets. So make a Twitter list where you can keep track of the critical businesses and people you want to follow.

### Use relevant hashtags

Twitter started the whole trend of hashtags, and other social platforms now have adopted them. Relevant hashtags are the best to keep you noticed on Twitter. They are a way of grouping tweets and putting them into a categorized box, making it easier for interested people to find you. Taking advantage of hashtags will make you gain more views, more followers and engagement. Enter keywords related to your brand or the popular hashtags that will help you grow your business

## *Set a tweeting strategy*

Within the 140 characters allowed on Twitter, you have to write something interesting, and engaging that covers a variety of different subject matters. This is a great marketing strategy to grow your business. Engage your audience with information about your business, link in your "About Me" page with a link to your business website, write about your product and services, the benefits and features of those. But you should also engage your audience with industry-related news and how-to guides related to your services.

## *Consistency*

This is the most critical Twitter strategy because

Twitter works on the top timeline and when you first tweet your tweet will be on the top of the timeline, but as other people keep tweeting, your tweet gradually gets pushed down and disappears to the bottom. Post regularly to keep the audience engaged and your posts at the top of Twitter. Consistency indicates professionalism.

### *Use an automated process to upload*

This will help you in case you don't have a robust and disciplined marketing team. Posting continuously in a day while handling a business can be a tough task. That is why there are ways to automate that process with social media automation tools. Hootsuite, Buffer, Sprout Social and other automation apps can be a great help to organize your post and keep the posts coming. It will help publish things for you when you are busy with other parts of your business.

### *Follow relevant people*

Follow people who are within your industry and are going to be interested in your content. Be selective about who you are following. You will automatically receive the right sort of followers as well who will be interested.

## Brand and identity

It is imperative to be clear about your brand and identity. You have some opportunities to put your brand out onto your Twitter profile. Your Avatar picture - where you can put your personal name or your brand name - your website address and a short biography. You can create your banner image that you feel reflects the brand and use this in all of your social media accounts, to maintain some consistency. This could be your company logo or personal headshot but make sure it's consistent across all your social media platforms.

## Differentiate whether you are promoting yourself or your business

This will help you in setting out a profile that is your core business strategy. Ask yourself whether you are promoting yourself or the business. Are people coming to your business through you? Or what is the link there? If you are primarily faceless within your organization, then you do not need a personal Twitter account. You can make it all about your business.

## Use the SEO benefits

The main benefit of using Twitter to grow a business is that it has also got SEO benefits. Here you can drop links to your websites, and you can be found easily. Twitter gets boosted into Google page rank, which means that you can appear in Google search engines. This also allows networking quickly with other businesses.

## Find niche leaders

First, you need to find people's Twitter accounts that talk about your niche, create a Google Adwords account and use keyword planner tool. Once you find these keywords, look up those keywords, make a list of top clean keywords, plug this into Twitter to find and follow the accounts. Engage with the niche leaders and they will open lots of digital doors for your business.

## Manual Twitter follower generation

This is a way to get followers organically on Twitter using the manual technique. The basic principle is finding niche-specific accounts and finding their followers. Pay attention to their followers and follow followers who you know are genuinely interested in your niche.

## Write eye-catching headlines

This is the first step for anyone to click on someone's tweets. We all have the habit of clicking on the most compelling and exciting headlines of any news, so write clever headlines. There are apps on the market these days that help you write the perfect headlines.

## Use Twitter analytics

This will analyze and optimize your tweets. You will understand how many audiences engage in your profile. Your analytics will help you keep track of your marketing performance.

## Get more creative than your competitor

Twitter is all about getting noticed; so creative

tweets always get the most attention. Take a sneak peek at what your competitors are doing on Twitter and do better by using your strengths. If you are good at videos, make Vines for your tweets. If you like to build a relationship, create an awesome influencer-marketing event. If you are good at photography, share your photos. If you like poetry, you can always share a haiku. You get the gist.

Most important of all the above points is to become a part of the Twitter community, offer help and be of value. This is the quickest way to grow your audience organically and also once you do this, the entire process will seem natural. Send really valuable tweets to engage your followers and gain more in the process.

**Your Quick Start Action Step:**

Step 1: Set up your brand on Twitter. Use your brand logo as the profile picture and use the profile header to tell a short story about your brand. Select a username as close to your brand name as possible and keep it simple.

Step 2: Complete the Twitter profile details. Add a link to your blog or website. Add a location, which tells people where your business is based. Also, add information about who you are and what your brand does in the Bio section. Give it some personality so that people are attracted to your brand.

Step 3: Follow other Twitter users. Be selective and don't follow too many people at once. You can follow people by going to their profile and clicking on the "Follow" button. This will allow you to see their tweets in your feed. Opt to follow your loyal customers, business partners, competitors, organizations from your industry, and people in your professional network. Check your email address list to see if your acquaintances are on Twitter and follow them. They are most likely to follow you back too. You can also organize your followers into separate lists. This allows you to see tweets on different pages according to groups. So create a separate list for customers, leads, businesses, etc.

Step 4: Start talking on Twitter. If you have a

brand campaign planned, start tweeting accordingly. Twitter is much faster-paced compared to other social media. Tweet messages related to your campaign. This will be visible to anyone who follows you. Reply to anyone who messages you. You can also reach out to followers via private messages. Retweeting is like reposting, so do this when you notice something interesting or a tweet relevant to your brand. Be smart when you tweet and talk less but adequately. Make sure you answer any questions about your brand. Add images related to your brand, product, and services in your tweets to attract more attention. Adding photos on Twitter is not as stressful as Instagram so you can be less professional about it. Use hashtags to expand your audience. Select hashtags related to your topic and create new ones for your brand.

Step 5: Drive traffic to other platforms. You can add a link to your website, social media profiles, and blogs in your tweet. A URL shortener can be used to keep the link short. Make the tweet interesting so that it compels the viewer to click on the link to know more. Add links to other social media profiles in your Twitter profile or tweets. This will allow users to view all the content you post on the web. You can send followers from one platform to another by doing this.

# Chapter 11: Guide to Creating a Brand Logo

# Chapter 11: Guide to Creating a Brand Logo

## 11.1 Plan Before you start

Be as descriptive as possible when planning about your logo design. Note it down on paper; remember that you want your logo to give your brand a personality, and to do that we need to understand your brand's personality. Once you have a clear idea of how your brand is unique from the rest, it will be easier for you to design the logo. There are a few questions you need to ask yourself to understand the personality of your brand.

## 11.2 What is Your Business About?

What are the types of goods and services your business provides to the customers? What is essential for you as a company? What are the core beliefs and values that your company follows? What makes your business unique? How do you describe your business? How do you want your buyers to describe you as a business? How do you want to be presented to the world? These are a few things that would help you reach the roots to what your brand personality would look like.

### *Be inspired*

Creating anything without any inspiration could be hard. So it is vital to stay motivated while making your logo.

You can brainstorm with the people who are involved in your business; people always help make it easier. Doing it alone can be stressful and confusing, so always set meetings where you and your partners and other teammates can brainstorm together. You will be surprised how they will help you out of the confusion. The more perspectives, the better it gets. Write down all the ideas even if you think it is awful. Bad ideas can make a great solution sometimes, and it always helps to develop the train of thought while brainstorming.

Be your customer, think like them and think of what they would need and appreciate and what would serve them of value. Make a note of how you want your brand to help the targeted audience by placing yourself in their shoes for whenever you feel less inspired.

### *Create a mood board*

This also is a perfect way of keeping you inspired. Collect images of what inspires you for your brand and stick them all in a board. Imagine a big board filled with all your tastes to give you a different perspective on your style. Think of your business and what your logo needs to represent. If your business is something related to organic foods and services, then try and look for something related to your brand. You may like a luxurious looking effect or more down to earth vintage style for your business, so think about what your taste and what your business is trying to convey to the respected audience. Your mood board will help you understand when you put all these inspirations together.

### *Look at the logos used by your competitors*

This is another best place for you to get some ideas for your logo. Look for your competitors' logos; do not steal their style if you like it, but be inspired. Also, check on logos of brands that are not doing well and try to figure out why. You will most likely see why the winners are on the top if you stalk them well and do good research on the business. Think of what makes you different from these businesses and always try to be unique from your competition. If most of the business logo styles are the same monochromatic effect, then you can be bold and go for a vibrant red to stand out. If everyone has a modern styled logo then maybe you can go for a more traditional style, this is the fastest way to attract attention and set yourself apart from the rest.

### *Choose a style*

Now that you have brainstormed, looked for inspiration and found some styles that you like, choose your style. It is time to start creating these styles into a design for your logo. Do not get overwhelmed with creating the entire design at once; take it one step at a time. The shapes, colors, typography, and graphics are all the elements that come together to give you one whole design. So pay attention and choose which color you would like then move on to select the right graphic, typography, shapes, etc. Choose what you think is best for your brand and always remember the kind of audience you are targeting at each step and make a choice accordingly.

*A classic style*

Trendy logos as the name suggest are here only for the trend and will be exciting and fun only for a few months then they will quickly start to fade. A classic will help you reach the broader range of audience, something beyond your targeted audience because a classic is something that suits everybody and will never get old. It is aesthetic and straightforward and doesn't go crazy on colors, fonts or graphics keeping the design as minimal as possible. If you do research on logos, then you will see the majority of the brands that are doing well in the world all have one thing in common: They have kept their logos as simple as possible. A classic style is safe and reliable.

*A vintage style*

There is something aesthetically pleasing about vintage looks. You are instantly reminded of the past and olden days. These types of logos have been trendy for quite some time, and it has been great for some brands as logos. The moment you see a vintage retro design, a feeling of nostalgia evokes inside of you, and this is precisely how these designs attract customers. It tells the customers that history is important to them, and it just somehow feels cooler to buy a product that looks old with worn out handwritten logos. It gives a sense of a very old brand even when it has been around only for a year or two.

*A minimalistic style*

This has been popular in this generation where people are more aware of minimalism. Brands often choose a minimalistic style showing the customer that your brand is new and well informed. The minimalistic style is clean and fresh with a lot of modern elements in it. Lots of whitespace, simple lines or simple, neat logos are what people are aesthetically attracted to. So they are trendy as well and appealing to the eye.

*A quirky and fun style*

If your brand's targeted audience is young or young-at-heart customers, then you have to keep them in mind. Chances are, your brand will catch their attention if your logo is fun and quirky with colorful fonts and fun style. You can use symbols and make it very energetic or give a friendly vibe radiating positivity. A cute mascot or happy illustration will display your brand's fun and quirky character.

*A handmade style*

Handmade is a more severe approach, which tells the customer that your brand stands for handmade quality. This style goes well with vintage and minimal styles. Handmade can give the customers a clear message that the brand is all about handmade crafts and the interested or targeted customers will understand and be attracted at first glance.

*A mix and match style*

When you find yourself confused between which styles to choose, mix everything up, and it would give you a different style. Your brand can be both modern and vintage at the same time; this will make you stand out with your creative idea.

### *Use monograms*

This can be helpful, especially if your brand name is very long. You can use the brand initials and still be known as a brand. This is also very minimalistic and although they may not be very informative about the brand, they still give out a good short name that people would remember.

### *Try wordmarks*

Wordmarks are typography used for brand logos. They are simple and give a straightforward message to the consumer talking about the brand; this works for brands with unique names. It provides the brand with some personality and is easy to recognize.

### *Make it pictorial*

These are the kind of logo we think about. They are images made to represent the brand to be easily recognized. It can be a straightforward pictorial logo or an intricate iconographic image, but make sure you try to make it as unique as possible, something that would stand out from the crowd. They are sometimes paired with word mark so customers would know the name of the brand. And sometimes they are not paired with any typography, for example, Apple. People know it's an apple product the moment they see the logo, and that is very amazing.

### *Abstract and geometric logos*

Abstract logo falls into a different spectrum of logos; they are sometimes unrelated to the brand itself. They create something unique and different for the brand. It looks very modern, and it is doesn't necessarily connect with the brand, giving the entire brand a different look from what the brand is. There are meanings to different kinds of geometric shapes you can always create a mood or a feeling by using the abstract logo to your brand. These are not recognizable symbols, so it helps a lot in standing out. You can use this step when you want to stand out and give a unique feeling to your brand.

### *Use mascot designs*

Mascots are for family-friendly brands. They make the customers perceive that your brand is very approachable. The mascots are colorful and fun, so they go well for children brands and family restaurants as well. You can use this for your brand if your brand has a younger target audience.

### *Use a combination mark*

Combination marks are a combination of words and symbols together in a logo. The brand name is placed near the symbol of the brand. It makes it easier to remember the name of the brand. This type of logo is commonly used and makes an excellent logo for any kind of brand.

### *Create an emblem*

The emblem is similar to a combination mark. They consist of texts in a symbol. Emblems are found in badges, crests, and seals; even silver or gold buttons for coats and shirts. They give a certain class to a brand. They are classic and old-school, vintage in appearance. Use emblems to provide a classic appearance to your brand.

### *Pay close attention to colors*

Colors have different meanings and they have certain emotions attached to them. Pay attention to the kind of colors you choose for your logo.

*Red*

This color stands for passion, excitement, and rage. Red will be a great choice if your brand has a target audience of young people. It is loud, bold and stands out

*Orange*

This is very vibrant and is not used as much as red, but this playful color is a very good choice for a more relaxed yet youthful audience, as it is a very energetic, playful and strong color.

*Green*

This color is very versatile so it can work for any kind of brand and audience. However, it works great for people who are connected to nature.

*Blue*

This is one of the most classic and popular colors. It is calming and gives a very cooling effect. Blue symbolizes trustworthiness, maturity and purity. Blue can be a great color choice for toddlers as well as the aged audience. It is very fresh and a common choice for most when choosing a color for their logos.

*Purple*

This color is feminine and very luxurious. There are a lot of shades for the color purple. It is a mysterious, vibrant and gorgeous color. Most brands with a female target audience opt for this color.

*Pink*

This is a very kiddie and girly color. But with other shades of pink, it can also be a very mature color, with shades like pastel rose. A brand with a female target audience commonly uses pink to attract their customers, and nothing can ever work better. Pink is a very youthful, feminine and delicate color.

*Brown*

Brown works for masculine, rugged, vintage-themed logos. It will give your brand a very rustic and handmade or aged look. Brands with male or older target audience can go for brown colored logos, as it is a very mature, sober and neutral color.

*Black*

Nothing beats black. Black is the simplest yet the most sophisticated color. It gives a sleek, luxurious, minimalistic and modern look to a logo; it is another widely used color for logos. It is a very neutral color, which does not seek much attention, but it still stands out. If you want to keep your logo design as simple, black is the best color.

*White*

This color is the cleanest of all, giving your logo a very modern minimalistic look. It works well with all the other color hues combined because it is a neutral color. It provides a very youthful, pure, clean touch to a logo. It can be utilized for any type of logo to keep it looking fresh.

*Grey*

This color is for a sophisticated, serious and classic look for your logo. It is a very mysterious and sophisticated color. It is dull, but it is fun at the same time. This works best if you want to send a message of seriousness and classiness together.

## Combine colors for your logo

You do not need to stick with just one color. You can use several combinations of colors together to bring a completely different look. These are the colors that go well together.

*Complimentary colors*

Colors that are opposite to each other in the color wheel are the complementary colors, for example, navy and orange, blue and red. They work well together and bring out the very best in both the colors to bring about a dynamic look.

*Analogous colors*

Colors that fall next to each other are the analogous colors. They give a sense of harmony to your logo when used together as they synchronize and go well together.

*Triadic colors*

Colors that are comparably spaced around the color wheel while making a triangle are the triadic colors. These three colors that fall at the end of the angles of each line of the triangle are great colors to create a bold look for your logo.

## ***Typography***

Always choose the right typography. Pick a font that complements your logo color, symbol, or the picture in the logo. There are four basic kinds of fonts that give unique looking logos.

*Serif fonts*

Use these to create a very vintage, elegant, old-fashioned and classic look. They look timeless and very high quality. Good for logos that want to be perceived as a classy and high end.

*Sans serif fonts*

These are perfect for the modern day clean look. They are minimalistic and go well with modern brands. They look neat and clean. Great for logos that want to look modern and outgoing.

*Script fonts*

These are handwritten fonts. They are calligraphic and give your logo a very relaxed and down to earth look.

*Display fonts*

These are decorative fonts; they are very stylish and flamboyant. They are eye-catching and look perfect for logos that want to be perceived as fun with retro feels.

### Bring it all together

Now that you have understood the different elements of your logos, you need to make sure they all go well together. They should all be combined in a very harmonious way. Combine all the elements according to how you want to create your logo for a fresh and unique look.

### Get your designer and communicate

If you are not the designer for your logo, make sure you have excellent communication with your logo designer on how you want your logo to look. Make everything as clear as possible for the designer to understand. Give them details about your brand and trust your designer to deliver what you want them to. Try to work together and give clear feedback on the progress.

## *Get some feedback from friends*

This is when you need to step out and reach out for people around you for honest feedback on your logo. This step is to evaluate your logo; here are the few questions you need to ask:

- Can you tell me what this business is about judging the logo of this brand?
- Is it a simple logo to memorize? Will you remember the way it looks?
- Is it timeless?
- Is it unique?
- Does it look appealing? (To your targeted

audience)

Now that you have discovered how to create a logo and all the elements involved in making a logo. Your business is ready to show its new face to the world. You have also learned the ideal basis of creating a design for your business, whether it is to create a business card or packaging design. Once you have a logo, your brand is now ready to start.

## 11.3 Quick Tips for Creating a Logo

1. Use logo templates or logo makers. If you want a quick way to create a logo design, this is the way to go. There are various websites and software that will give you thousands of logo templates to work with. You can build and adapt from this starting point.

2. Try to avoid any cliché's. Ignore the trends. Avoid using any logo idea that many others have already used. This will not help you stand out and be unique in a crowded market. Thinking of original logo design will work to your benefit.

3. Avoid creating a logo that is generic and will likely be copied by others. Create something new and unique that you can lay complete claim on. When someone sees your brands logo, they should not confuse it with any other brand.

4. It may not be alright for you to whip out some amazingly intrinsic design, but your logo can still be significant. Does the Apple logo look like a complex design with unique fonts? It still is one of the most well-known and unique logos out there. You can keep it simple and effective too.

5. Try to keep proportion and symmetry in mind.

6. Using negative space can help you add another unique dimension to your logo. The FedEx arrow is a classic example of this.

These are some tips given by professional logo makers, and they will help you create a brand logo that does not fail to grab attention.

# Chapter 12: Building Brand Loyalty

# Chapter 12: Building Brand Loyalty

## 12.1 What is Brand Loyalty?

Have you noticed that you, your family or friends tend to go to the same stores all the time? This is an example of brand loyalty. People tend to continuously purchase products from the same brand all the time, regardless of other competing brands. If your brand builds a good relationship with consumers, you can create a strong sense of brand loyalty among them, and this is an important aspect of branding. This brand loyalty will help generate regular income for your brand and increase customer referrals.

## 12.2 Importance of Brand Loyalty

Brand loyalty is important because it helps businesses to push past competitors and gain an advantage. It is important to nurture this loyalty to succeed in a large marketplace. When a company has strong brand loyalty, their customers will keep buying their products over the years. They will disregard any change in packaging, increase in price, or even new products once they establish trust in the brand. They will trust the brand to deliver high quality and useful products or services. If you instill this sense of brand loyalty, your consumers are less likely to be swayed by marketing gimmicks from competitors. This means your brand can stand strong even in the face of adversity with the help of these loyal customers. Establishing a loyal following also helps increase the customer base over time. When people see others trusting a particular brand, they are inclined to trust it too. One person's satisfaction will gain you the trust of many more. Brand loyalty will effectively work as costless advertising for your business.

**12.3 How to Develop Brand Loyalty?**

With so many new brands and products being offered every day, what can make your customers stand by you? The answer is brand loyalty, and you need to help your customers develop this.

The following tips will help you build brand

loyalty in an extremely competitive market.

## *Quality first*

The initial thing to bear in mind is that you should not compromise on quality. Your products or services should not fall below the standards set by your competitors. You may not offer something extremely different, but it should be of good quality nonetheless.

## *Customer engagement*

The second pointer is always to engage your customers. Keep in touch with your customers and let them know you value them. Keep sharing new content with them and communicate with them as often as you can.

## *Listen to your customers*

Take feedback from your customers and show that you care about their opinions. Everyone likes to feel important, and if you provide this to them, they will want to support your brand. Provide your customers with what they want if you want them to stay loyal.

### *Incentivize the customer*

Provide incentives to customers to come back to your brand. If they purchase something for the first time, offer a discount code to be used on their next purchase. They will not want to let the opportunity pass. Also, create loyalty programs that award them points according to how much they shop.

### *Keep up with the market*

Stay updated with current trends and be relevant in the present market. Don't use old strategies that don't work in the present day.

### *Appreciate the customer*

Show appreciation to customers and send them automated messages to wish them well on birthdays and holidays. This will make them connect to you and appreciate your service.

### Your Quick Start Action Step:

Create a schedule to carry out the steps given in the section 'How To Develop Brand Loyalty?'

# Chapter 13: Putting It All Together - How to Launch A Branding Campaign

# Chapter 13: Putting It All Together - How to Launch A Branding Campaign

## 13.1 About Branding Campaigns

If you look out in the world today, you can easily see why brands are more prominent now than they ever were. The products or services your business provides will have a life cycle. However, a strong brand can outlive any of these product cycles. You can use your brand to convey consistent quality and build credibility. Your customers will know that your brand provides a unique and dependable experience. So regardless of what product you provide, they will continue to be your consumers.

Grasping the concept of a branding campaign is essential. By definition, it is a part of brand management that aims to develop a brand with the help of communication with customers. The tips given on social media marketing in the previous chapters have to be integrated into your branding campaign. The objective of a brand campaign is to differentiate the brand and its products from its competitors and to convince customers of its value. Like we mentioned already, brands are essential at this point. There are various reasons for this, and you will learn why brand campaigns are essential in the next section. The point is, the whole world is online now, and the market is continuously growing. Consumers are present everywhere, and they all want to buy branded products. Premium brands are more attractive, and people strive to buy more from these. So if you want to be a successful business to consumers, you have to have a strong brand as well. Having a strong idea will help your brand in the best way possible.

If you look at the popular advertisements, you will see that the brand has created its campaign with remarkable creativity to appeal to its customers. This kind of strong campaign helps to garner attention and creates interest around your brand. If you want an active brand campaign, you need to think outside of the box. A normal brand building strategy has to be combined with the cultural movement strategy to accelerate the growth of your brand. This will allow you to maximize the impact of any steps you take in your campaign. Brand campaigns don't have to be extremely expensive anymore to be successful. If you have a strong creative team, you can take advantage of all the new tools available and grow your brand rapidly.

## 13.2 The Importance of a Well-Planned Branding Campaign

It is crucial to use a well-planned branding campaign for your business these days. It would be insane not to utilize all the online marketing mediums available at this point. Ignoring online space can cause imminent failure. The different components of a successful campaign should focus on building your brand.

## 13.3 How to Launch a Branding Campaign

### Create a brand logo and tagline

Think of any popular brand that you like, and their logo will instantly come to mind. Most of these brands also have a catchy tagline that they tend to use while advertising or marketing their products. For example, Nike's tick symbol and "Just Do It' tagline will be recognized by nearly anyone in the world. These taglines and logos are unique to such successful brands and its high time you create one for your business as well.

Step one is to know why you need a logo and why you need it to look great. Business is all about attracting the right customers, so you need to think of a logo that goes according to who you're trying to attract. The logo is significant because it is the face of your brand. The services and goods that your business provides are qualities that add to your brand, but your logo will be a first impression on the customers. Your logo has a huge impact on the perception of your business, it will speak to the customers about the company, and if it is the right business for them. A great logo can make you stand out in this competitive business world. At the end of this chapter, we have added a guide to help you create the perfect logo for your brand.

## *Develop a strong brand identity*

Before you focus on the tangible elements of brand identity, you have to identify what your brand stands for. There are different questions that you need to answer to understand who you are as a brand.

- What is your brand's mission?
- What are the values or beliefs that drive your business?
- What is the personality you want to portray as a brand?
- How do you intend to create unique positioning among all the competition?
- What is your brand's voice?

The answers to these inquiries will define your brand, so you have to grasp an understanding of each of these elements fully. Don't be worried about this particular process because you will figure it out. You have to ask yourself simple questions like why you started the business in the first place and what makes you different from others. You also have to keep your values in mind and think of the way you want customers to perceive your brand. After you have figured out the answers to all these questions, it will be simple enough to start working on building your brand identity.

## Getting started with building a brand identity

The brand identity of your company can be built based on your design. Design assets are tangible elements that will give a specific image to your brand. This includes logo, tagline, web design, packaging, business cards, social media graphics and even the uniforms that your employees might wear. Therefore, nailing your design can be nailing the most visible aspects of your brand identity.

First, you have to develop your brand design. You have to start from the ground up while doing this. The building blocks of your brand identity begin from here. These include elements like typography and color palette.

Typography is the fonts you use for all your

branding materials.

The color palette is another essential factor to consider. Colors have different psychological associations, and you can make use of these differences according to what image you want to portray.

Form and shape should also be considered while creating designs. These are subtle but effective elements in reinforcing certain desired reactions. For example, round shapes create a feeling of community and love. Squares or rectangles give the image of strength and stability. Straight lines are more masculine and mellow. So choose the desired shapes carefully and balance them out with the right colors and fonts.

Now you have to design your brand identity. After figuring out the building blocks, you can enlist the help of a designer and start to bring things to life. You have to translate all your ideas into a tangible brand identity. Various elements can be used for expressing brand identity, and these will depend on the type of business itself.

The following are the prevailing elements of a brand identity:

- Logo
- Website
- Product packaging
- Business cards
- Email design

After you have figured out all these brand assets, they have to be used most effectively. Create a brand style guide to help you with this. A brand style guide document will outline these design elements and how or when you should use them. It will also inform you what you should or should not do in terms of design. You can use this document over time and generate the right image with your audience.

### *Guidelines for creating a brand identity*

- Step one is to ensure that you have a complete brand strategy ready. You can focus on brand identity once your brand strategy is set up and documented.

- Understand what brand identity is and why it is essential. The information given in this chapter should have helped you in this to a large extent.

- Do sufficient research before you dive into the design aspect. You need to understand the audience you will be reaching out to and figure out the best way to connect with them. Every phase of a branding project should be approached and worked on in detail. Create a persona for your brand. This is what the world will see when they look at your brand. Identify who your competition is and make your brand more unique and visible. Examine the current state of your brand and make any required changes while developing positive aspects further.

- This is where you build your brand identity. You have enough information by now to work on reaching the ideals you have in mind. Work on the elements mentioned in this chapter. The brand logo is one of the most crucial aspects, and the next chapter will help you in detail on creating the best logo and tagline for your brand.

- Build an appropriate and practical brand style guide that will allow you to use the designed brand identity in the best way possible.

## *Campaign goals*

First, you need to think clearly about what you hope to achieve with your brand campaign. Don't invest in advertising or other meaningless actions before you do this. It will be hard to assess the success or failure of a campaign until you set your campaign goals in advance. It is critical that your campaign goals are measurable. For instance, if you want to achieve a specific growth, check on the number of visits that increase on your page. It is not easy to define the objectives of your campaign, but it needs to be worked on. A briefing needs to be clear and agreed upon by everyone involved in the brand campaign. A typical campaign can take anywhere between 3-6 months for completion. In this time, you have to interact with the team and check on progress continuously.

## *Target audience*

Use data mining to understand your customers. Conduct studies to find what your target audience finds interesting and is looking for. Use analytical tools like Google Analytics and Facebook analytics for customer segmentation. It will help you gain insights that will help in every aspect of your campaign.

## *Campaign budget*

You have to determine the amount of money that you will be spending on the brand campaign. This budget will have a direct impact on your campaign, as it will determine the actions that you can take. For instance, a small budget will not allow you to spend on television ads. However, you don't have to stress about this because a low-budget campaign can still be extremely useful if carried out the right way.

Think about the most effective ways to reach out to your clients and spend money only on those actions. You have to spend a little on campaigning, but it does not necessarily have to be a considerable amount. Allocate the budget carefully so that you can ensure that the right audience is being attracted.

### *Select the right marketing medium for your brand*

Different types of marketing campaigns are available, and they will depend on where the consumers spend their time. You have to invest time and research to determine which type of marketing is best suited for your specific brand. The following are the essential marketing methods used these days:

**Internet marketing** - Your brand being present on the Internet itself is a type of marketing by itself.

**Search engine optimization** - SEO is the process by which you optimize the content on your website so that it appears when consumers search for specific results.

**Search engine marketing** - It is slightly different from SEO. You can pay a search engine provider to place links to your business on pages that get a higher number of views.

**Blog marketing** - A blog is not just for an individual who wants to write. Various brands have started using blogs as a way to connect to their customers.

**Social media marketing** - Everything from Facebook to Instagram is available for businesses to create a lasting and positive impression on their targeted audience. Social media is also a great way to connect and conduct business directly.

**Print marketing** - A business can sponsor articles or different types of content in magazines and newspapers according to their specific audience.

**Video marketing** - It is not just about commercials anymore. You can now invest in the creation of different types of videos that will entertain and inform your audience.

All of these are great marketing methods that will be crucial to the success of your business.

## 13.4 How to Decide on the Right Marketing Strategy?

Now that you know so much about marketing, you are probably confused about which strategies you should use for your business. These tips will help you to figure out what will work best for your business. But as you keep reading, you will understand why we emphasize the use of social media marketing for your brand.

### *Determine your marketing goal*

First, you have to determine what your marketing goal is. What is the purpose of marketing your product or service in the first place? Are you aiming for more leads or just trying to increase brand awareness? These questions will help you decide on specific marketing techniques.

### *Select your target audience*

It is vital for you to recognize who your potential

customers are. Keep them in mind and determine the best way to connect with them. You have to consider what mediums they prefer and how best you can communicate with those specific people.

### *Create a budget for marketing*

Set aside money that you can afford to spend on marketing. This is the budget within which you have to work. Initially, it is hard for smaller businesses to spend a lot on marketing, but this amount will increase as the business grows. Don't spend more than you can afford. Your marketing strategy will rely on how much you can afford to spend on it.

### *Keep the location in mind*

Some marketing methods work better in certain areas while they perform poorly in others. You also may have to target a specific area if you are a location-specific business, like realtors.

Although there are various marketing methods available, you don't have to rush into trying all of them. Think strategically about what you can afford and which will work better for your particular business. If something doesn't pan out, you can try another way.

## 13.5 Create a Plan of Action and Execute It

Make a list of what you have to do and allocate time for each of those actions. Don't focus on making this too elaborate. It should just be like a to-do list that you can tick off as you complete each task. This list will be like a record that you can use for evaluation when your campaign is completed. For example, if you are launching a branding campaign on Instagram, your action plan should consist of the following:

- Think of the content you want to post.

- Convert these into real photos or videos to be posted.

- Plan a schedule for when these will be posted on Instagram and assign dates and times for each post according to data analytics.

- Have captions and hashtags ready for

these posts.

- Promote this campaign via other mediums.

This is just a simple example campaign plan to carry out. You can stay organized by ticking off each task that you complete in your plan. It will provide you with a sense of accomplishment, keep you motivated, and help you track your progress.

**13.6 Measure Your Result**

Measure the results of your campaign, improve on it and repeat the process for better results. Once your actual branding campaign is carried out, you need to take time and study the process and results. Check the goals you had set initially and see if your campaign helped to achieve those goals. This will be a measure of the success of your campaign. You can then use the results of this campaign to make decisions about future campaigns. It will help you learn what worked and what needs to be changed or improved. If you paid for a specific form of marketing, check if it paid off for you. If not, refrain from using that medium again or find a way to make it work next time. If some other medium worked for you, invest more money in that in the next campaign. You need to build on whatever brings your brand the maximum benefits. Repeat the process and look for continuous improvement and more significant results. This is how successful branding campaigns work.

**Your Quick Start Action Step:**

You have to schedule a time where you can focus on studying then applying the steps on launching a branding campaign.

Step 1: Understand your target audience. Conduct sufficient research to help you understand the customers you are targeting. Position your brand in a favorable light for them. Taking time to understand their lifestyle and spending habits will help. You need to identify the people who will be interested in purchasing products from your brand.

Step 2: Start creating social media profiles for your brand according to the ones that your target audience uses the most. Social media marketing is essential for your brand campaign. A strong social media presence will work in your favor, and you need to be willing to spend time and money on this. Create, curate and post content that is visually appealing for your audience and will convince them to follow your brand.

Step 3: Use digital marketing to increase the effectiveness of your brand campaign. This includes marketing on social media, websites, search engines, etc. Pay-per-clicks is one way of marketing your brand.

Step 4: Pay attention to the public relations aspect. Your brand will stand out and gain more coverage if you use the right public relations tactics. Hire professionals to spread your campaign in the most effective ways and get results. Use PR initiatives to the advantage of your brand. When something doesn't work, find another way.

# Bonus Chapter: When is it Time to Rebrand

# Bonus Chapter: When is it Time to Rebrand

## 14.1 When to Consider Rebranding?

Don't shy away from the thought of rebranding. It has become an increasingly common approach that has benefitted many companies over the years. Consumers don't usually notice this rebranding unless it is carried out massively. Subtle transformations like color changes in logos are also considered a part of the rebranding. However, no matter how small or large scale the actions, the intent is serious. Rebranding shows a commitment to grow and evolve as a brand, and it can be a way to convince your consumers that your brand is evolving with time and staying up to date and relevant.

If the following apply to your business, it might just be time to rebrand.

***If you want to shake off a particular image***

Sometimes a brand may be associated with an

image that does not benefit it over time. It can be something that deteriorates the value of the brand. In such cases, rebranding can help your business win over a new image in the eyes of the public. Take time to learn about the rebranding of Burberry as a case in point. Would you believe that this high-end brand was once associated with thugs?

## *If you want to focus on a new demographic*

Sometimes you need to tap into a new audience for the growth of your business. At this time, you have to rebrand in a way that appeals to this new audience. Do the required research and find the right market while capitalizing on a different demographic.

## *If you want to stay relevant*

If you feel you have outgrown the original mission statement of your brand. When the market changes, you need to offer something different and show that the brand is still relevant.

### *If the market is changing too quickly*

To stay competitive in an evolving marketplace, you may need to rebrand. This will prevent you from being left behind by competitors who are continually building on their brand image to keep up with times.

### *If your brand name is all you have*

In this day and age, a name is not enough. Visuals are important, and great branding is required for your business to stand out and survive. Rebranding can help you gain back your status and grow.

## 14.2 Importance of Rebranding

Many times, companies find themselves losing their standing because they ignore the signs. Not employing rebranding at a strategic time can mean the failure of your business at times. The following pointers will help to convince you of the importance of rebranding:

- Companies can lose their reputations when their branding strategy is not clear or due to some unfortunate instances. Rebranding can help to restore the trust of people at such times.

- Lack of proper branding can result in the ineffectiveness of campaigns and thus, loss of money. Effective rebranding can solve this problem, which will result in successful marketing.

- Internal efforts often take a long time to complete when the branding message is not consistent. A strong rebranding message will help to recreate an effective branding strategy.

- You cannot translate the value of your brand to consumers if you don't have a clear brand image. It will prevent you from identifying your consumer's needs as well.

Rebranding can help your business kickstart an entirely new image. It is important to adjust the brand image according to customer needs if you want your business to thrive.

## 14.3 How to Rebrand

Rebranding may sound intimidating yet fun to many people. However, rebranding is crucial that it should be done correctly since it can make or break your brand too. The fun parts of rebranding are much smaller than the significant changes you will need to make.

### *Research*

To start with, do the research. Understand your brand and analyze your customers as well as the market. Don't be hasty in rebranding. Do the same kind of research you need before you even begin branding your business. The answers to those initial questions might have changed over time. Your customers might need different things now, and your community might have a different view of your brand.

### *Communicate*

Take time to communicate clearly and effectively with all stakeholders in your business. Tell them what the key objectives of the rebranding will be and inform them of the planned timeline. Also discuss the budget, positioning changes, and implications for each department. Everybody should be on the same page.

### *Document*

Document everything that is planned and being carried out during the rebranding process.

### *Plan effectively*

Roll out the plan effectively. This stage needs to be carried out well for the investment to be worth it. Use PR campaigns or launch parties as you see fit. The rollout for each brand can differ owing to various factors.

### *Stay strong as a brand*

Defend your brand at every turn once the rebranding is complete. Show people that your brand is strong and can withstand any hurdles.

### **Your Quick Start Action Step:**

Create a plan and schedule a timeline for the entire process of rebranding. Set the time required for conducting research and then create a plan from the analysis. Then create a timeline wherein you have to execute the plan of action for rolling out the new brand image. Stick to this action plan and execute every minute detail effectively.

# Conclusion

Thank you again for choosing this book!

I hope this book was able to help you to understand more about branding and marketing. You can see why branding is important for your business and why you need to start investing money in this. I hope you also have enough information to guide you with social media marketing now. In this digital age, it is crucial for brands to keep up with the latest trends and move according to the masses. This is the only way to grow and promote your business.

The next step is to follow all the call to action steps given in the chapters and act on building your brand. You need to make use of all the information presented in this book and make it work for your brand. It will help you surpass your competitors and consistently take your business to the next level.

Thank you and good luck!

# References

Why marketers must set business goals. (2019). Retrieved from https://exchange.cim.co.uk/editorial/why-marketers-must-set-business-goals/

Smithson, E. (2019). What Is Branding And Why Is It Important For Your Business? | Brandingmag. Retrieved from https://www.brandingmag.com/2015/10/14/what-is-branding-and-why-is-it-important-for-your-business/

How to Define Your Target Market. (2019). Retrieved from https://www.inc.com/guides/2010/06/defining-your-target-market.html

Facebook Ads: The Complete Guide to Getting Started with Facebook Ads. (2019). Retrieved from https://buffer.com/library/facebook-ads

The Complete Guide to Advertising on Instagram. (2019). Retrieved from https://www.wordstream.com/blog/ws/2017/1

1/20/instagram-advertising

Definition of Rebranding | What is Rebranding ? Rebranding Meaning - The Economic Times. (2019). Retrieved from https://m.economictimes.com/definition/rebranding/amp

History of marketing. (2019). Retrieved from https://en.m.wikipedia.org/wiki/History_of_marketing

Nichols, J. (2019). Council Post: Eight Tips For Rebranding Your Company. Retrieved from https://www.forbes.com/sites/forbescommunicationscouncil/2018/09/25/eight-tips-for-rebranding-your-company/amp/

Facebook. (2019). Retrieved from https://en.m.wikipedia.org/wiki/Facebook

The Brand Integration Moment is Now Part I. (2019). Retrieved from https://www.thedrum.com/industryinsights/2018/07/16/the-brand-integration-moment-now-part-i

Team, K., Team, K., & Team, K. (2019). 5 Ways

To Promote Your Brand On Twitter | KWSM: a digital marketing agency. Retrieved from https://kwsmdigital.com/5-ways-to-promote-your-brand-on-twitter/

Long, J. (2019). 7 Marketing Tips to Help Grow Your Brand on Instagram. Retrieved from https://www.entrepreneur.com/amphtml/280964

Facebook, H. (2019). How to Promote your Small Business on Facebook. Retrieved from https://www.businessnewsdaily.com/5453-how-to-promote-your-small-business-on-facebook.html

9 Tips for Promoting Your Brand on YouTube | AllBusiness.com. (2019). Retrieved from https://www.allbusiness.com/9-tips-for-promoting-your-brand-youtube-99022-1.html/amp

Brand Loyalty: What You Need to Know. (2019). Retrieved from https://www.investopedia.com/terms/b/brand-loyalty.asp

Lashuk, A. (2019). 7 Tips to Promote a Brand on YouTube. Retrieved from https://www.templatemonster.com/blog/7-tips-promote-brand-youtube/

What is Brand Loyalty - Definition, Importance with Examples | Marketing Tutor. (2019). Retrieved from https://www.marketingtutor.net/what-is-brand-loyalty/

Duckler, M. (2019). Rethinking Your Brand Position's Target Audience. Retrieved from https://www.targetmarketingmag.com/article/rethinking-your-brand-positionings-target-audience/

How to Create an Authentic Brand Story that Actually Improves Trust. (2019). Retrieved from https://neilpatel.com/blog/create-authentic-brand-story/amp/

Brand Story | The Story of Telling. (2019). Retrieved from https://thestoryoftelling.com/brand-story-services/

Allbee, C. (2019). 10 Steps to Building a Brand to Reach Your Target Audience. Retrieved from https://www.impulsecreative.com/blog/10-steps-to-building-a-brand-to-reach-your-target-audience?hs_amp=true

12 Essential Rules to Follow When Designing a Logo | Webdesigner Depot. (2019). Retrieved from https://www.webdesignerdepot.com/2009/06/12-essential-rules-to-follow-when-designing-a-logo/

www.ingramcontent.com/pod-product-compliance
Lightning Source LLC
Chambersburg PA
CBHW051542020426
42333CB00016B/2057